INTO THE

ANTIQUITIES

TRADE

INTO THE

ANTIQUITIES

TRADE

KEVIN R. CHEEK

This book was printed in the United States of America.

To order additional copies of this book, contact:
Xlibris Corporation
1-888-795-4274
www.Xlibris.com
Orders@Xlibris.com
21453

CONTENTS

For Wendell,
for He found the first coin.

PROLOGUE

My father, God bless his soul, was a good and kind man. He always delighted in giving my sister and me a special present for the holidays and this Christmas holiday was no exception. My mom and dad had just returned from the Bahamas from their yearly winter vacation and as usual, they were bearing gifts. My mother had already gift-wrapped our presents and I couldn't wait until Christmas morning to open the small package that had my name on it.

I had just returned from my first trip to Germany and little did I know that trip would be the first of many in my future. Like every tourist, I saw my share of castles and beer halls, but what fascinated me the most about the place were all the small and quaint mom-and-pop gift shops. I found that I enjoyed going through them and discovering their treasures. One might say that I had a sense of the hunt, which I found I began to enjoy more and more. Perhaps this stemmed from my upbringing in western Kansas, where every fall we would go out en masse and hunt pheasants with various shotguns of all descriptions.

Once in a while, we would also go out and look for arrowheads in the open fields. We would sometimes find a nice specimen in places where the wind would blow out a sand hollow or a shallow depression. After a few hours of scanning the ground, I was able to train my eye to the ground and I was able to find more and more pieces. I never knew it at the time, but this was my first taste of the *hunt*.

Christmas Day finally rolled around and it became time to open my present. My curiosity was heightened by the small size of the box, as it was the size of a ring box. Like a kid, I shook the box to see if there was any movement inside. Nothing moved that might offer me a clue. I resigned myself to open the box as quickly as possible. Removing the top and eagerly peeling back a layer of cotton, I revealed what looked to be a round object that looked like a military metal. Upon closer inspection, I held it up into the light and I could see that it was a silver coin.

This coin was unlike any other coin that I have ever seen or handled. Its planchet was thick and bulky, and its diameter was about one inch. What struck me the most about this coin was the fact that it was rather heavy and appeared to be extremely old. The surface had a tarnished patina from age and did not look like the shiny money that we see every day. The coin also appeared to have some wear on the high points of its relief and this contributed to its beauty and mysterious eye appeal. The design was powerful and magnificent, with the profile bust of a young and strong-looking man who was wearing a lion's skin headdress. The reverse of the coin featured a muscular figure seen on a throne, holding out a standing eagle and behind the throne was an inscription. The legend was in Greek letters, and when translated into English read, "A-L-E-X-A-N-D-E-R."

My father then looked at me and said, "This coin is over 2,300 years old and was minted by Alexander the Great in 323 B.C. There is a symbol seen below the throne on the reverse that indicates that this coin was minted in Babylon. Do with the coin as you wish and Merry Christmas!" he exclaimed.

I was stunned. I began to think of who might have possibly handled the coin over the years and how it could have survived down to our time. The ancient city of Babylon, I recalled from my high school history class, was Alexander's imperial capital and the place where he died. Was this coin minted shortly before or after his death? Why was this coin made? What was the meaning of the lion's skin headdress? Who was the muscular and bearded figure seated on the reverse? In time, I would be able to answer many of these questions because now I was hooked. I had now discovered a hidden world of history and passion, and I was to learn that this was a world where people had played for keeps, and in this world, the gods set down their rule of law. I had now entered a world from which there was no return; from this point on I had become a collector and in time, I would become a dealer.

I found the world of antiquities was unlike any other business. It is a network of dealers, collectors, sources, middlemen, academics, restorers, bankers, and runners. Some would say it is a world of drug kingpins, charlatans, grave robbers, smugglers, and money launderers. Others would say it is a world of hardworking people who share in a trade where money is made with a particular piece, from its source to the collector. Everyone, even remotely connected with the trade, has a different viewpoint about its inner workings and this viewpoint would always be slanted as to who we are. In truth, the essence of the antiquities trade is a service that meets a demand with a product like any other business, but what sets it apart is the *nature of the product itself* and because of this, there are all sorts of people that are engaged in the trade, both honest and dishonest, both legal and illegal, and both legitimate and illegitimate. The trade will always continue to flourish as long as there is a desire to collect and the desire to collect has been evident since the dawn of recorded history. Layers upon layers of regulation and red tape will not deter a true collector from collecting; in fact it will only push his or her desire even more, and through it all, prices tend to rise. This point has been proven over the last twenty years with the exploding prices seen on the international market. High prices have driven more people to dig up pieces, in order to feed their starving families, especially in countries that have a low GNP per capita and a high unemployment rate.

The politics and opinions regarding the antiquities trade are endless, and at the beginning of my career, politics and opinions did not enter my mind, and the thing that did enter my mind from the very start was the beauty and eye appeal of the objects themselves. This is all that matters to most collectors, and to be honest, enjoying the beauty of the objects and their preservation is still what is really important to me.

Over the years I have seen one inescapable fact, and that fact is that there is no better protector and preserver of antiquities than the private collector.

Most collectors are proud of their collections and go to extra lengths to purchase custom stands and sealed cases. There are many museums worldwide that fail to treat their objects as well, and often store their hundreds of duplicate pieces in boxes, sometimes in a basement where no one sees the pieces for years. I was surprised to find many well-known public institutions that have bad plumbing, nonexistent atmospheric controls, unstable display cases, and water dripping through their ceilings. All of these factors play havoc on their collections and contribute to their rapid deterioration.

I can remember seeing the King Tutankhamun exhibit in the Cairo Museum in 1984 and many of the large gold pieces were still displayed in many of the original wooden and glass cases that were built shortly after Howard Carter's discoveries in 1922. The exhibit was on the second floor of the museum, and upon seeing the famous golden death mask, I could hear the traffic on the street through the open windows that were a mere ten feet from the display case. This fact stuck in my mind a full fourteen years later when seeing the fabulous golden death mask again and I could see that the gold appeared to have lost some of its luster. My suspicions were confirmed when I compared my close-up photos from both visits.

The close-up photos were taken with a high magnification lens and a Nikon 35-mm camera. I even took into account that the paper from the earlier photos might have tinted somewhat due to age, but a redevelopment of the photos seemed to confirm what I was afraid of, and that was that the air pollution in Cairo appeared to have been acting on the surface of the metal. The museum certainly wasn't airtight and no effort was done to make it so. The air pollution was making its insidious way into the museum and working on the pieces on display. The death mask appeared to have developed some noticeable oxidation on the surface. The oxidation would naturally affect the metal pieces in the museum first, then possibly the textiles and the stone sculptures over a longer duration of time, as is the case with the Parthenon in central Athens. The obvious solution to this problem would mean moving the Cairo Museum into a new facility, preferably in the country where the clear arid air would act as a natural preserver, but obviously this would take a great deal of money to build a new facility and perhaps, it would also make it harder for the mass of tourists to view the collection.

My last visit to the museum was in 1987, and perhaps by now the museum officials have upgraded the air filtration system in the building and built new display cases, replacing those old glass and wooden cases that were used for all those years, but after viewing the photos, other questions came to mind. Did the museum curators leave the King Tutankhamun exhibit all those years in those old cases for visual effect for the tourists? Could it be that that the Egyptian government does not want the museum to move out of the city and sacrifice the potential entry fees that they now collect at the door? Those fees are into the millions per year, in addition to the fees that they charge for their archeological sites and other provincial museums scattered throughout the country. Could it be that this scenario is just the tip of the iceberg, and that there are many governments that could be guilty of trading the condition and preservation of their antiquities for money?

An analogous situation could be seen at the famous site of Chichen Itza in the Yucatan peninsula in Mexico. This site is perhaps the most famous in Mexico and is only a few hours by car from Cancun. The images of the Temple of the Warriors and the El Castillo are in most of the tourist brochures of Mexico. My first visit there was in 1982 and one can see numerous huge glyphs or stelae that were built into the sides of many of the buildings. The primary building material for the Maya is the native limestone that was easy to carve with great detail. These magnificent carvings would usually display a standing figure with a series of glyphs that would denote a time and/or event. The black and white pictures I took of the site were detailed, with contrasting grays that brought out the minute features of the carvings. The depth of the carvings could be seen and a dramatic 3D effect could be seen on many of them.

I was totally devastated during my revisit in 1997. Many of the glyphs had been worn down by the hordes of tourists that the Mexicans had run through the site. Many of the glyphs were completely worn down, beginning from a low point where it was easy to reach down at the knee, to a high point of reach above the head. Most of the wear could be seen at chest level and graduated less and less, as one reaches further up above the head or further down at the knee. Many tourists are unaware that their hands have oils and other bodily fluids that can wear down limestone with constant touching of the surface. In this case, I came to the conclusion that this is a clear case of a government trading the condition and preservation of their archaeological sites for money.

The 1970 UNESCO accords (Convention on the Means of Prohibiting the Illicit Import, Export, and Transfer of Ownership of Cultural Property) that many of these "art-rich" countries have agreed to, are intended to protect their archaeological sites, but it is a sad reality that tourist dollars may have become the greatest enemy to the preservation of many archeological sites worldwide. How the "art-rich" countries use those tourist dollars to preserve their sites and museums often takes a back seat to the political agendas and economic needs of the populace. Protecting a "cash cow" is the line of argument that many governments have taken, and in the process, have attacked the concept of the private collector as a protector and preserver of antiquities.

Through my experience in the trade, I found that most private collectors contribute to our knowledge of a particular culture. Many private collections are on loan to several museums and are published in academic journals and exhibition catalogs. Many private collectors have also collaborated with archeologists relative to an academic work and/or specialized type of study. This is especially true for die studies regarding ancient coins, because there are different die combinations and coin types that can be seen for a particular mint, or mints, over a specific time frame and geographical area. A great deal of coinage would be needed for an academic publication of this type, in order to link the various die combinations and identify the various weight standards.

Private collections have added immensely to these types of studies for the simple reason that many private collections have a great deal of the scarce to rare material. Some of these coins are so rare that they can only be found in old private collections and in some cases, these collections date well over a hundred years. The private collector that understands the importance of these academic endeavors is usually very happy to contribute, and in many instances, notwithstanding financial reasons, winds up donating their collections to a public institution.

Private collectors are responsible for many of the great museum collections that the public now sees worldwide. There are those in the academic community that think private collecting is selfish and illegal, but I personally think that no one should have a monopoly over art and/or say who can or can't collect.

It is my view that art is a universal form of expression that no one, including governments, individuals, and institutions, should have a monopoly over.

I have decided to tell you, the reader, about my experiences in the trade so that you may decide for yourselves if people should be able to freely collect antiquities, and if the archaeologists are right in their thinking that they should be the only ones that can handle and excavate ancient objects, and if the current international rules and regulations are fair relative to the collectors, dealers, public institutions, archeologists, and the governments involved. The critics of this work may also contend that financial gain is the main reason I have decided to reveal some of the inner workings of the trade to the public, and this is true to some degree, but the primary reason I decided to go forward with this work stems from my concern about the continued *private* preservation of ancient works of art.

In summation, for those of you that are lovers of ancient art and history, it is my sincerest wish that people today have a better idea as to what the antiquities trade is all about, and that the public may see that there are always two sides of the coin, contrary to what one often reads in the press and what government cultural ministers, archaeologists, and politicians have to say about the trade.

CHAPTER ONE

The Quest for Knowledge

Harlan J. Berk examined the coin over and over again. He looked at it under high magnification with his pocket loop and concluded that it was authentic. The high relief signs of wear were visible under the glass, along with the minute flecks of spotty black manganese. The coin was a small tetraobol that was minted, circa fourth century B.C., in a small city in northern Greece named Terone. This denomination was used primarily for everyday trade, such as a purchase in the local market or *plaka*. Terone was known for its wine exports and the obverse of the coin naturally featured a wine amphora. The coin was not worth much and Harlan's interest had not yet peaked in the deal. He snorted his approval as I offered him the next object in the package.

Harlan was a typical midwestern coin and antiquities dealer who was no-nonsense and right to the point. His slightly portly physique was misleading, for he was a powerful man who a few years before our meeting was able to complete a marathon race along with his attractive lithe wife, Pam. Harlan was also one of the few individuals where his brain matched his body, and he always had an uncanny sense of what was authentic and what was a cleaver fake. I always admired him for this ability, although once in a while his rigid opinions would get in the way and cloud his judgment.

The next object was a gold Greek Hellenistic ring that had a flat face. Engraved into the face was a standing Nike, the Greek goddess of victory. She was seen leaning forward holding a victory wreath aloft with one arm and her body was sheathed in flowing drapery that seemed to portray eternal movement, which is a Greek Hellenistic form of expression. The Nike seemed to convey a feeling of eternal youth, and it was as if it was saying that:

"I am immortal and victory itself is within me, may I grant it to you if you are worthy!"

The piece had multiple minute scratches all over the surface, which was the norm for an ancient gold piece such as this, and I knew Harlan would see this through his pocket loop. A sudden burst of energy appeared to flow through Harlan and I knew then he wanted the piece. I also knew he was attempting to conceal his interest in the piece by flatly remarking, "How much?"

I calmly replied, "Five thousand dollars." Harlan knew that he had a good bargain. The ring would sell for over $13,000.00 on the open market in the US. Harlan made an offer for the coin, the ring, and the other objects that were pure junk. I pondered for a moment and then nodded my head in approval. Harlan dished out $7,000.00 in crisp cold cash and I shook hands. I was happy with the deal, because I was able to move the junk and quickly turn the pieces over.

Smiling, he patted me on the back and said, "Please come again."

I waved farewell as he was closing the door to the elevator hallway and I blandly said, "See you in a few months."

All at once his face went from cheerfully roguish to visibly troubled, almost anguished. "I did not really get that good of a look at that ring, my eyes are not what they were. The light was bad in that office," he said with some anxiety.

"Don't worry about the piece," I said.

I could see that Harlan still appeared to be a little uneasy and I added, "I got a good look at it outside in the light of day.

The piece had some patina with some mint frosting over the gold."

Harlan then relaxed and I said with a smile, "Does this mean you are going to buy at *Carson's Ribs* for my next visit here to the windy city?"

"Smart-ass." Harlan replied.

Later ensconced in my hotel room, I was pleased. Relaxing back on the bed and staring at the TV, I was happy Harlan had faith in me not only to buy package deals, but also deals that were mixed. Harlan was a dealer who was one of the top dealers in the world for ancient coins. He sold coins worth millions of dollars per year and knew each and every coin, but more importantly, he knew his customers even better. He worked hard in his trade and started from a small coin shop in Joliet, Illinois, then worked up to a gallery on Michigan Avenue, and then a few years later, purchased offices across from city hall on Clark Street in downtown Chicago. I knew that by working with Harlan I had arrived in the trade and that there would be many more deals for me in the future. I also realized that I could learn a great deal from Harlan. Some of his fellow numismatists accused Harlan of having an overbearing ego, but deservedly so, as his depth of numismatic knowledge regarding history, weight standards, stylistic nuances, and minting techniques were considerable. For a man who was middle-aged, he had gone far.

During our meeting, I recalled he commented on his new theory, *The Master Die Theory*, that proved that a number of Greek mints during the classical period, circa 408-336 B.C., employed a mint master that cut the dies for a proof issue. Subsequent die cutters, who may or may not have been trained by the master, would then copy this proof issue. His theory was based on artistic style and the examination of hundreds of coins for that specific mint. Only years of experience and the constant examination of new issues, which would suddenly appear on the market, finally made this apparent to him.

For Harlan to form his theory, he was in a position that no

archeologist could ever be in, and that was to see everything firsthand. The world of archeology needed men like Harlan, because the dating of ancient coinage ties everything together at a dig site, especially when a coin is found in a known ground stratum. I felt that those that shunned dealers like Harlan, only because he was a dealer, were making a mistake. After all, isn't the quest of knowledge about ancient cultures really what archeology is all about? With that thought in mind I drifted off into a deep sleep.

The following week, I decided to take a vacation by jumping on a plane to Thessalonike for a visit to the famed Museum of Thessalonike. The gold Greek ring I sold Harlan spurred my interest in ancient Greek art and so I thought a visit there might be worthwhile. The featured exhibit had its origins in a small sleepy village in northern Greece named Vergina. I found that the exhibit was as interesting as the real story behind the find that made world headlines. The find put northern Greece in the spotlight and Thessalonike, the second largest city in Greece, became more noticed in travel magazines.

In 1977, the Greek archeologist, Dr. Manolis Andronicos, moved the first spade of dirt from a large round hill that he thought might possibly be a Macedonian burial mound that is known as a *tumulus*. The sheer size of the mound was deceptive and many thought that it was not man-made, but the wily Dr. Andronicos thought otherwise. His thinking was that this large mound was part of a sacred burial site and that it was possibly later expanded and enlarged by Antigonos Gonatas, circa 274 B.C. The plundering of the royal tombs by the Galatians a year earlier drove Antigonos to look after and protect the royal tombs of his ancestors. Dr. Andronicos thought the Great Tumulus was enlarged for this reason and his suspicions were heightened in 1962 when he found fragments of several grave steles, which is an ancient grave marker. Dr. Andronicos surmised these grave steles were from the surrounding cemetery and may have been broken in antiquity by the rampaging Galatians, and they were used as fill to increase the size of the mound. Dr. Andronicos was to later find that the tombs he discovered were not centered directly below the center, but rather off to the side. This would make it extremely difficult for someone that was digging straight down from the center to find anything. Antigonos Gonatas was clever in adding to the size of the mound in this fashion.

Dr. Andronicos thought at the time in 1962 that this site might have been the original Macedonian capital named Aigai, although its origins had been pure speculation. He concluded that his answer might be in the Great Tumulus and he began a large-scale excavation there in 1976. The sheer size of the mound made it necessary that he use earthmovers, along with the normal basket-by-basket method of removing the fill dirt. Once he got down into the mound, through a series of test trenches, he discovered a group of tombs with one containing a large gold ossuary with the sixteen-rayed Macedonian royal star on the top lid. Inside this wondrous box were a gold wreath and the charred bones of a man who is now thought to be none other than Philip II, the father of Alexander the Great.

His bones were later laid out in a simple glass case at the Museum of Thessalonike and the signs of battle were readily evident. The years of forging a ragtag country into a nation with a formidable army had taken its toll. Philip's eye socket had been damaged along with one of his legs. Philip II was thought to have lost his right eye to an arrow during his siege at Methone in 355 B.C. and damaged his leg several times in battle. The skull in the case revealed trauma around the right eye socket. British researchers in 1984, including Dr. Jonathan H. Musgrave, senior lecturer in anatomy at the University of Bristol in England, contended that a bump above the skull's right eye socket was a healed-over wound. A pair of bronze shin greaves, which wrapped around the lower leg and provided protection in battle, were found in the tomb and were made with one shorter than the other which would accommodate a man's leg injury. Considering the rich gold and silver vessels that were also found in the tomb, the wide array of weapons, and the signs of hasty construction of the tomb's main chamber, most experts are in agreement, including Dr. Andronicos, that this was indeed the tomb of Philip II.

The gold and silver objects were dazzling in the museum, but it was those bones in that simple glass case that had the greatest impact on me. They seemed to be crying out from the case:

"I am who they say I am and grant me only one wish . . . let my memory live on!"

I think this was the museum's greatest moment and, really, they should be commended for showing those bones the way they did. That simple glass case surrounded by all the glitter of gold and silver objects was truly a stroke of genius, and the end result was a very powerful display. Collectors of classical antiquities know that sometimes it's not the most dazzling objects that are the most important, but rather the simple objects that can tell the tale, and in this case, those simple objects were the bones of Philip II himself. The head director of the Museum of Thessalonike, Aikaterina Rhomiopoulou, did Philip II some justice in creating a display as bold as the man himself, and along with the world-famous grave goods that were found, the birth of the modern state of Greece is a story that can best be seen in those bones.

Thinking back, the Greek gold ring seemed to push me forward and it revealed to me a key element of the antiquities trade that became apparent to me with my visit to the Museum of Thessalonike. What I began to realize and understand was that what separated the ancient Greek culture from that of other ancient cultures was their constant search for knowledge and the condition of man, and in an analogous context, the quest for knowledge is really what the core of the trade is all about, from collectors striving to learn more about their objects, to the dealers who strive to learn more about the objects they sell, and behind every object there is a story, and this story is the raison d'être as to how and why it came into the modern world.

Like the tomb of Philip II, it took an able mind to understand the story behind its discovery. I had now had a clear path before me and I decided that now was the time to start making some discoveries of my own. There could now be no turning back for me, the die was cast as to what direction my life would take, and that direction pointed to a world many generations gone by. Many stories would be revealed to me, for many objects were also on the horizon.

CHAPTER TWO

Into the Void

The airplane arced its way over the rugged landscape below. The two plus hour flight north from Karachi was uneventful. There was nothing to be seen, nothing but a vast wasteland of desert and half-dead plants. As the plane landed, I could see the heat radiating off the tarmac and the barren landscape. A stray dog ran across the runway and off into a drainage ditch at the edge of the airport perimeter. So this is Peshawar, arms bazaar of the world and financed by our CIA to who-knows-what degree.

From the air, Peshawar looked like the mud brick capital of the world, unlike its Sanskrit name meaning "city of flowers." The city was a mix of countless modern mud brick structures and the older, but sturdier, old stone fortresses and bazaars built centuries ago. On the edge of the city was a sea of tents that housed the thousands of war refugees from Afghanistan. From the air, they resembled small dark gray and black dots that were embedded in a tan sea of sand that seemed to flow away from the city.

Exiting the plane, I was the only passenger without a turban. Talk about feeling out of place! Walking down the air stairs, I got a good look around and there were twenty Pakistani guards with automatic weapons guarding the plane. Their green berets and thick camouflage jackets with kevlar lining told me that these were the guys that you did not want to mess around with.

Once I got into the plain cinder block terminal with its distinctly dirty yellowed white tile, I was overrun by twenty taxi mongers who could say nothing but "Taxi! Taxi! Taxi!"

I decided to pick the young one with green teeth and tattered *Jordash* designed jeans. I figured that maybe he would work harder for me because he was younger than the rest. I didn't check my bags and I had only carry-on. A quick exit from the airport was preferred.

Walking fast and quickly and looking around in five directions at once, young green teeth gasped and finally set his eyes on me, "My name is Merhdad; are you from California?"

"No, Merhdad. My name is Kevin and I am from Colorado. Where is your car?" I quickly asked, as I gave my shoulder bag another tug to secure it during the fast walk. I had $2,500.00 in cash in that bag for my first big antiquities deal. Today in New York that amount would not go far, but back then, that cash was a king's fortune in this part of the world. I concealed my nervousness and focused on the airport parking lot that was filled with dilapidated Ford Falcons.

Merhdad began to wave impatiently, his right arm moving in circles like a windmill on a breezy day.

"This way! This way! See it's the white one there." He pointed to a dirty white Ford Pinto, or at least it looked like a Ford Pinto. What struck me about this car was that it seemed not to be bolted together, but had all sorts of wires and welds that all brought the various pieces of the vehicle together. The welds were about one-half inch thick and they looked solid. In fact, the car was a conglomerate of parts and it was surprisingly complete because of all the welds. My only worry was that the Pinto was known to have an unstable gas tank that was prone to explode. One good hit from behind and we were toast. I learned later that this car had quarter-inch armor plating welded into the body, so as to flatten any bullets on impact, and a custom suspension to handle the added weight to the car. My fears were unfounded about the car; it was in fact a mini-armored personnel carrier.

On the way to my hotel, I could see that the war in Afghanistan had taken its toll on the people. Everywhere I looked there were refugees that had missing limbs and horrid shrapnel wounds. There were people with wounds that were unimaginable. The Russians had changed their tactics in 1981 and began a policy of wounding, rather than killing the civilians. They would dump hundreds and hundreds of plastic kidney-shaped antipersonnel mines from airplanes. They would scatter like leaves and arm upon impact. Their small flat shape and light gray color made them extremely difficult to see, because they all looked like a small stone. The children would take long sticks and constantly tap the ground ahead to detonate the mines when traveling along the pathways and trails. These mines would be powerful enough to blow off a foot and there were many children with missing feet in Afghanistan and Peshawar. It was no wonder that an estimated six million refugees had fled Afghanistan and were living in neighboring Pakistan and Iran. They knew that each step you take in the path of war is death.

It was against this background of war that I hoped to make a deal. I was looking for Kushan gold staters and Greek silver tetradrachms. This part of the world was at the furthest reaches of Alexander the Great's empire. After his death in 323 B.C., Seleukos I, who was one of Alexander's generals, gained control of the region and it subsequently broke away as an independent kingdom known as Bactria in the third century B.C. The Greek Hellenistic coinage of the Indo-Greek Bactrian kingdoms was remarkable in that they produced coins with extremely realistic portraiture. These coins resembled a photograph of the rulers and they always had a wide planchet or flan. One of my favorites was a coin minted by Eukratides I, circa 170-145 B.C., that showed a barebacked king holding a raised spear and wearing a pith helmet. What makes this coin so special is that this monarch's back is seen towards the viewer and he is looking back over his shoulder towards his target. The flexing muscles in his back convey a young and vigorous ruler that was capable of holding his own against his enemies. This coin is a Greek masterpiece of art and I felt I had a shot at finding some. Rumor had it that the Afghans were melting the coins down into silver bars so they could more easily sell the metal. If I could save some of these coins for posterity, then perhaps someday I could say that this trip was worth it. There was a good chance that the seller couldn't even afford a Band-Aid, and it would be a good feeling if I could put some money in his pocket so that he could buy some food and medicine for his family.

The international rule of law does not apply here and the rule of law is by the end of a gun, and in Afghanistan with the Taliban now running the show, owning a gun is symbolic of a young man's passage to manhood. In this part of the world, one could say that a gun is definitely man's best friend.

Under the Taliban regime, the people have not fared well and many have died from freezing in the winter and malnutrition. They pack tightly into whatever shelter they can find to keep warm. The women have no rights and their social standing is below that of a pack animal. Everything is bought and sold by barter and the Taliban control the food supply. Perhaps that is their true hold over the people, rather than their religious Islamic rule of law. It is my prediction that many more will die there, perhaps in biblical proportions in the near future.

What people have failed to understand, about this part of the world, is that not much has changed in the thinking of the people since ancient times, and one could call this convention of thought an *ancient mentality.* One case that perhaps illustrates this is seen with Iraq's Saddam Hussein, who often paraded around on a white horse while shooting a revolver into the air, and the analogy of Hussein with his revolver and Eukratides I with his spear is quite evident. In ancient times, as well as today, it always took a perceived strong leader so that some degree of control could be maintained over the populace. A society could then thrive that often conducted business by barter and this in turn, would give rise to mini-fiefdoms that to this day, still control the economies of many countries in the region.

Ancient superstition and ceremony have also survived in the more remote reaches of northern Pakistan and Afghanistan. There are pockets in the Hindu Kush region of northern Pakistan where the people still speak Greek and have a deep self-pride in being descendants of the earlier, ancient Indo-Greek kingdoms. The Kalash people there have blue eyes and fair skin. They still worship a pantheon of gods, make wine, and practice animal sacrifice. They have no part of Islam and are a thorn for the Islamic government of Pakistan. One could argue that it is these people who have a more legitimate claim to their ancient Greek heritage, i.e., *cultural patrimony,* than the current Islamic government of Pakistan. Their resistance to convert to Islam is steadfast and they want nothing to do with the current Islamic society and religious beliefs.

Given the close-knit cultures here, I realized for me to do a deal I would need some allies. Why not start with my guy here? Knowing Merhdad was probably Sunni Muslim I yelled, "Hey, Merhdad, let's go into the nearest bar and have a soda pop!"

Merhdad looked into his rearview mirror and smiled. Those now familiar green teeth presented themselves again, within his rapidly moving head that was moving up and down like one of those plastic dolls that one often sees hanging from a car's rearview mirror while in vacation in Mexico.

He quipped, "OK, OK-hot day, no drink much. OK!"

The car sped in front of an open building that had no ceiling, two walls, and tables that were randomly spread out. Merhdad braked hard and pulled up into a space that ran in front of the building. It was full of old men playing cards for small change that were all smoking Camel cigarettes without the filters. I suddenly realized why Merhdad had dental problems; it was probably from all those years of smoking without any filters and most likely, he started when he was young. I was glad that I had brought twenty cartons of American cigarettes for making friends and to trade for objects. I was to later find that those cigarettes would be more valuable than gold and could buy more objects than any U.S. greenbacks ever could.

Taking a seat at a table that was welded together like Merhdad's car, the old guys didn't pay much attention to me and I began to feel more relaxed, so I decided to find out what made this guy tick by asking a few questions.

"Merhdad, how long have you driven this car?" I asked.

"Five years, Kevin. I drive car five years. Save money. Make car from parts. Car good. No big problems. Strong moto," he said.

"So, you see many Americans here in Peshawar? Has business been good for you? You also speak some English, no?" I calmly asked.

"My mother teach me some English. Some Americans here, not many. They bring weapons for war. Teach mujahideen how to work. I do OK. Make money with American who take photos. I drive him everywhere. I also sell fuel for cooking. What you here?" he asked with an open-eyed look with the green teeth showing.

It was a clever response. I now knew Merhdad was as interested in me as I was in him. He suspected that I needed him for something and I decided I needed to start somewhere and gain his trust.

"Merhdad, I am here to buy old coins and objects. Very, very old, and that's why I am here, not what," I said with a hushed response.

Merhdad's eyes now became even bigger and he said, "Yes, I know what you mean. German man come to look for same. I take him to find in Afghanistan. Village north of Towr Kham. Much danger. See many mujahideen with Russian prisoners in chains. They come to trade." He said while always waving his hands and every word he spoke was always accompanied with a hand wave here, or a subtle pointing there. This sort of dance with the hands was in a way, very Italian.

I was shocked. Russian prisoners in chains? This place must be a bazaar and staging area for the war. This would be the kind of place to find what I was looking for. My mind began to race. What did the mujahideen do with the Russian prisoners? Trade them? Kill them? Or both? I thought this place would definitely not be in *National Geographic*, but would certainly be featured in *Soldier of Fortune.*

"Merhdad, what becomes of the Russian prisoners? Are they killed or traded?" I asked.

"Some killed, some traded, some let go . . . some die," He said, handing me a business card that read: "Car by Merhdad—Peshawar International Airport."

"Merhdad there is no phone number here," I said, as I put it in my wallet.

"No need phone, people know where to find me," he replied.

I suddenly realized that he was right-one can find anyone here simply by asking around, simply because everyone knew everyone here. That would make my job here a lot easier. Tribal and big family alliances had their advantages. Everybody had their place here in society, except for most of the women who had nothing except for their husbands. Their independent role in society was just beginning to emerge here in central Asia.

"Merhdad, I would like to hire you for the week. I want you to take me to this place. I will pay you five hundred dollars for your efforts and a bonus if I am successful. Is that fair and do you accept?" I asked.

Merhdad's eyes got even bigger and his mouth suddenly exploded in that huge green smile. Reaching for my hand to shake he said, "OK! OK!"

His handshake was firm and I knew I could trust him. This was important. Trust. My life could be in his hands. Somehow, I knew that he was a good person. He was hardworking and seemed to be willing to spend some time in helping me out. His life has been hard, but that is all that he knew. I knew then that I had the right man for the right job.

After downing a few Pepsi Colas without ice, Merhdad explained that the trip would take three days and we would have to walk in and out over the border. I was also a little amused to learn from Merhdad's comments that the German man was a terrible sleeper and he did nothing but complain.

I said, "Merhdad, there will be no complaints from me. I know what a trip like this will take. Let's travel light and get in and out fast. We will take some food, water, and some blankets to sleep on, nothing more, agreed?" Merhdad seemed relieved and shook my hand and nodded in approval.

"I would like to rest up for a day or so, do you know of a comfortable hotel?" I said.

Merhdad gave me that familiar smile and said, "Yes, one outside of town. Good one." Merhdad then drove me to the Pearl Continental Hotel that was at the time designed like an upgraded Hotel 6. The hotel had its own golf course that desperately needed water on the greens, which were a lighter brown from the fairways. I could hire a caddy for the expensive price of $6.00 for eighteen holes. I made arrangements for Merhdad to do some shopping in town for our trip and to have him pick me up the following morning. I thought it would be a good idea to let everyone at the hotel know that I was a photographer. I took a few pictures of the staff and a mound of half-buried brick rubble near one of the fairways.

I decided to play a round of golf and relax a little bit. Upon closer inspection of that brick mound after one of my typical errant shots, I could see that the bricks might possibly be well over a thousand years old. Who knows what was within this mound? Tomorrow morning, Merhdad was to pick me up and we would begin our journey into a country that few Americans have ever or would ever want to visit. I then hit a rare five iron shot four feet from the pin. I thought, as I walked up to the hole, that no doubt it would be dangerous; the best course of action would be quick in and out. I then promptly missed my putt to the right. At the end of the round, I gave my caddy ten dollars and he thanked me endlessly. I couldn't help but notice that his green teeth were somehow worse than Merhdad's.

The next morning, Merhdad was to greet me in the lobby

and he was there waiting for me when I came down to pay the bill.

"Good morning. Good morning, Kevin. Sleep good? Golf good?" he asked.

"Yes, Merhdad, sleep good, golf bad!" I said with a laugh.

"Let's have some breakfast and some strong coffee," I said.

On the way to breakfast at the hotel, I noticed that Merhdad had a green heavy jacket on that was of typical U.S. military issue.

"Good jacket, you were able to buy us these and everything else with no problem?"

"No problem, Kevin. I buy everything. No problem," Merhdad replied.

"Very good. Keep any money you have left over," I said, as I slapped Merhdad on the back.

Merhdad looked at me with that trademark smile and said, "Thank you, Kevin."

"Merhdad, no problem. It's important we have everything for the trip. Good job."

The mornings were cool here in Peshawar this time of year and the mercury begins to soar about 9:00 A.M. We loaded the car with my gear and I jumped into the front seat. Merhdad moved our new gear from the front seat into the rear seat and as he was doing so, I could see the cold flash of gray metal. He looked at me with a solid stare and said with a low voice, "This we may need." He then quickly lifted the cover of the bag, revealing a well-oiled AK-47 and he said with a whisper, "Do not worry. I will show you how to work it. Works good. You will see."

I then thought that to carry a weapon here was as normal as breathing air. Everyone had one, so why not us? It now sunk in hard just how dangerous this trip could be. I decided then to go for it and looking at Merhdad, I said, "Good, but use it only if you have to, OK?"

"OK, OK. No problem," he said, waving his hand like it was nothing.

The car leapt out on the only paved road out of town. We were heading west towards the Khyber Pass. We turned north at the Jamrud Fort and crossed the river at the Warsak Dam, then headed northwest. There were many armed mujahideen walking along the road and they all had weapons. It looked like they were armed with an assortment of handguns and the typical AK-47s. It was not hard to get a weapon here in Peshawar because every other shop was a gun shop. The gun shops were everywhere. It was like an old west town and there was no way Dodge City could compare. Peshawar could easily fit into a spaghetti western, and one of the few distinctions between the old west and Peshawar was that in Peshawar the weapons are modern and a whole lot more deadly, and it became obvious to me that not even Clint Eastwood in *Magnum Force* could have a chance here.

Looking more closely at the mujahideen, they were often seen in groups of three or four and they all appeared to be relaxed. I waved to several groups and they all laughed and joked around. They were not in a hurry and they were all friendly and wanted conversation. I did not see one Pakistani military policeman or soldiers from the moment we left Peshawar. My worry was that they might search our car and give me problems with all sorts of questions. I waved to several groups, took some photos, and they all laughed and pointed when they saw the camera.

The Khyber Pass was a mere 25 miles west of Peshawar. The pass had a colorful history with the most notable event being the battle of January 1842, during which 16,000 British and Indian troops were killed. It is doubtful if Alexander the Great himself had passed through this pass into India. Most historians are fairly certain that the bulk of his army of 75,000 went through passes in the Hindu Kush several miles to the north, probably the Shibar, Khaiwak, and the Salang passes that are west and north of modern-day Kabul. Could it be that Alexander sensed this pass could be a killing ground? If one looks at the map in the numerous publications about his conquest of the Persian Empire, one can see that he had a tendency to move over passes and routes that were not frequently used and were more secondary as a travel and/or trade route. The British could have learned from history, but military egos got in the way and their entire force was decimated in the Khyber, save one man who lived to tell the tale.

For the ancient Greeks, these passes were the main gateway into the Punjab from ancient Bactria. This is one of the main reasons why a great deal of ancient Indo-Greek objects and coinage have been found in the upper river basin of the Oxus, as this region is mostly west and north of these passes and is, in my opinion, the heart of ancient Bactria. This is the area where the ancient sites of Balkh and Ai Khanum are at in Afghanistan and where the mujahideen find many objects and coins. Ai Khanum is at the juncture of the Kokcha and Oxus rivers and upriver from the Kokcha is Asia's most famous mineral asset, the lapis lazuli of Badakshan's "blue mountain." This mineral was traded far and wide in antiquity and in ancient Egypt; objects made from this material were considered even more valuable than gold. Ai Khanum controlled the trade route for lapis lazuli and became an important Hellenistic Greek center, complete with a theater, baths, and temples with huge Corinthian columns. Its importance in antiquity should not be understated and many spectacular objects have been found there. The mujahideen did not lose sight of this and they would then bring objects and coins to the border with Pakistan in order to trade or sell them.

The village of Konar-e Khas was one such place, just inside the Afghan border, which is about sixty miles north of the Khyber Pass in the Kunar valley basin. Merhdad pointed out this place on my trusty Michelin road map and he explained we were going to an area just north of this village where an outdoor bazaar sprang up out of nowhere. I knew we would have to leave our car in Pakistan at some point and go by foot over the border. I was prepared for a three-day journey and a few nights of sleeping out in the open.

Merhdad had bought for me in town a few blankets, a green army jacket, and a backpack with some food and water. I was sure to pack my cigarettes and half my money. I left the other half of my loot and my passport back at the hotel safe in Peshawar. I planned to stay there on my return and take a long hot bath.

Merhdad traveled on the paved road for a short time and then he veered off the paved road onto a hard packed dirt road that went north. I could see the majestic snow-capped mountains of the Hindu Kush rising up from the plain. The border was at the base of the mountain range that ran about twenty miles away. The sheer size of the mountains was surprising and seemed to go north forever in the clear desert air. The car kicked up a trail of dust that could be seen miles away. The barren desert that had engulfed us reminded me of south central Colorado, where there is little plant life and one can see for miles. The road passed over many washes and gullies that looked like they would suddenly fill with water during a flash flood. There were many signs of erosion in the washes and gullies, along with bleached white animal bones that could be seen once in a while. At least I thought they were all scattered animal bones. I never really got out of the car to take a closer look. The heat was really starting to build and we rolled down the windows more to get more air. I could smell a sweet lilac scent in the rushing air and it was clean and pure. It brought to mind what T.E. Lawrence (Lawrence of Arabia) once said in the Arabian Desert in 1916 to an American reporter who asked, "What is it about the desert that grips you the most?"

And his reply was, "Because it is clean."

In a way I began to think of this place in the same way. The various broken down mud brick houses we would see once in a while were being worked on by the desert environment and they were slowly crumbling to dust. The environment was cleansing itself of anything that was man-made. When I looked into the weathered faces of the mujahideen, I could see an analogy that they too were being worked on by the harsh conditions of the desert and were slowly being crumbled into dust. The Hindu Kush has made boys into men at an early age and I could see that even the war took a back seat to this process. I thought that maybe I was lucky to see this place at least once in my lifetime. There was an exotic pull to this place and in a way it was like going to the moon, but there was also a downside, and that was if you made a mistake, it could be the end. I was determined to keep frosty from this point on and try to anticipate anything that might go wrong.

The mountain range became larger and larger as the road started to angle to the northwest. I knew that we were now close to the border. The mountains rose straight up from the plain and appeared to be at least three times larger than the Rocky Mountains and, as a skier, this was something that I could appreciate. There were snow-capped sections of the mountains that looked like daggers that were piercing the sky and as a whole, resembled a monumental fence that ran to the northeast against the barren plain for hundreds of miles and I knew then, with an unmistakable image and realization that would be forever branded into my memory—this was the Hindu Kush.

"Merhdad, how long do we travel north on this road before we get to the point where we leave the car?" I said.

"Three hours. No more. Park car and leave with guard. He stay with car. We go sleep in mountains. Walk in next day. Do most travel in night. Trail good and many people travel," he said with no worry. I could tell by the tone of his voice that this was for him a walk in the park.

Merhdad continued, "I go every few months to sell fuel for cooking. I know way well."

I suddenly felt a lot better about the trip. I had a feeling that this was a main supply route for the mujahideen and it was well-traveled and free of mines, but it also could be a primary target for the Russians and they might strike at any time, especially from the air.

"Merhdad, are there many mines?' I asked. This question weighed heavy in my mind as I remembered an article that I had read in *Newsweek* that there were an estimated twenty million land mines that were planted in Afghanistan, which is thought to be about one-fifth of the world's total active units.

"Yes, but mujahideen always look. New trail much danger. This trail always people look. No mines found. This old trail. Russians find old trail, then mujahideen make new trail. New trail danger. New trail many mines. Old trail OK. Mujahideen use many long sticks. Cover every foot on trail every day. Mujahideen say safe trail number one to win war. Move supplies. Win war," he said.

I thought for a moment that logistics were really the key to victory here in rugged Afghanistan. The mujahideen moved freely at night and their gray cloths made them look like rocks, as long as they didn't move. The Russians were pinned down except in the air. The static positions of their army made them easy targets. They were slowly being ground down into hamburger. It was only a matter of time before they bailed out.

Merhdad pointed up ahead to a small hill with a few mud brick houses. "Look there. Park car behind house. Leave with friend. He watch car. We rest and go tonight," he said.

By now, it was late afternoon and shadows began to get long. The Hindu Kush mountains rose up behind the little hill, forming a surreal canvas of purple and blue shapes with white tops. The car pulled up to three small mud-bricked houses and we were greeted by an excited barking dog that appeared to be well fed. He began to jump against the welded plates of the car looking for attention. This light brown dog was a Heinz 57 mix with some German shepherd. A man and a woman suddenly appeared from behind the nearest house and walked up to the car. Merhdad warmly greeted the couple and they were instantly focused on me.

"My American friend, Kevin. This is Ahmad and Joni. They my friends and guard car," Merhdad said. I extended my hand to Ahmad who shook it with a smile. Joni did the same and I said, "Happy to see you both. Do you speak English?"

They both laughed, shaking their heads, and they then began to rattle the tongue that was familiar to Merhdad. Merhdad said, "No speak. I speak for you. You third American they see. They happy you here. We can stay here tonight. They have warm house. OK?"

I replied, "OK. Let's stay and talk." Ahmad and Joni waved us into the closest house and they were all smiles. Following Ahmad into the house, I brushed the rug aside that that served as the door to the structure. The walls were surprisingly thick, perhaps as much as two feet and the roof was supported by huge crossbeams. The place reminded me of an Anasazi kiva that had few windows and one could feel the weight of the walls that surrounded and protected the family. The floor was covered with rich wool rugs that would belong inside any upscale mansion on Park Avenue in New York. One wall had a fireplace and there were rugs that were even hanging from the ceiling, which divided the house up into separate living rooms. All in all, the house appeared to be very comfortable and was unlike the impression that I had when first seeing it on the outside. Ahmad motioned for us to sit at a long wooden rectangular table that was coated with years of body oil and wear from use. Its thick parts were made from heavy planks and they were held together with iron spikes. I felt that the table should be in some castle in Scotland, rather than here in northwestern Pakistan. Something told me that Ahmad was doing well for himself in this barren area and I began to think of the ancient site of Ai Khanum, in that perhaps Ahmad also controlled his own little trade route into Afghanistan. Like the ancient site of Ai Khanum, Ahmad was profiting from the fact that his location facilitated trade.

I knew this analogy was true when Merhdad, after a long conversation with Ahmad at the table, turned to me and said, "Ahmad knows I have no fuel to sell. He asks why we go over the border. What do you want me to say?"

I said, "Merhdad, tell him the truth. We look for old coins and objects." Merhdad looked at me and smiled. I could see in his eyes that my answer was what he expected and that I was a man who did not want to deceive anyone.

I remembered what old Amil Sarkisian once told me after I showed him that coin I got for Christmas. "Trust. Build that and you can deal anywhere. Never forget it." he said.

Sarkisian was one of the old timers who brought objects out of the Middle East in-between both world wars. There was not a major museum in the United States that did not have any pieces that could be traced back to him. I knew him when he was in his eighties and he died at the ripe old age of ninety-three. He was originally from Armenia and he centered his operations in Beirut and began trading in carpets. From there, it was an easy step into the antiquities trade. Objects came to him along with the rugs. He later parlayed his sales into commercial real estate in Denver and made millions. I wish I could have known him longer. His knowledge of the objects is now lost, because his son Greg was only interested in learning about the carpets. I had a feeling that Sarky was a little disappointed in this, but I never brought it up with him.

Ahmad looked at me with a wry grin. He got up from the table and then returned with a small wooden box. Placing it on the table he began conversing with Merhdad. Merhdad then said to me, "Kevin, if you want what is in box, make offer. His brother find this two days ago near here. He knows it is old, worth money. You look."

I felt elated. I had spent three days here and already my first deal was staring me in the face. He pushed the box over to me and gestured that I open it. I opened the box and within it was what I never expected. There, inside the box was a Roman glass flask in the shape of a grape cluster and in the trade, this type of vessel is known as a mold-made *unguentarium*. It was in mint condition, without any cracks or chips, and was about four inches high. It was dark purple and blue, with multicolored iridescence that covered the outer layer of the surface. Some of this iridescence was flaking off and there was some sand stuck on the inner surface of the vessel. This sand could easily be removed with a small stick and would not be a problem, as long as I was patient in removing it.

The shape of this object was mesmerizing, not only because the main body was in the shape of a grape cluster, but there was also an opening at the top that was an elongated neck that had a lip at the end. This vessel probably held precious oil or perfume, hence its name unguentarium, and its design made it easy for the owner to control the flow of liquid from the one-inch neck at the top. This piece was mold-made and was rare on the international market, especially in this large size, as most specimens were half this size. It was probably produced in modern-day Syria during the A.D. first to second centuries, and found its way east without being broken.

What a piece! I stared at the purple and dark blue iridescence, realizing that this was the result of the outer layer of glass that was deteriorating, like the thin outer layer of an onion. As one moved the vessel back and forth, one could see brilliant hues that would burst forth into the light like a fine polished fire opal gemstone. This piece had developed a beauty on the surface that was unmatched by any modern glass object that could easily be found in any mail order catalog or store. Collectors, above all, value this patina along with the mint condition and I instantly knew this piece would bring a fortune in London or New York. The amazing part about this type of piece was that it was such a delicate and fragile object, yet it had survived since the A.D. second century in a hard and hostile land such as this, and finally came to rest here in this box. Even finding a piece such as this required the finder to take care in separating it from the ground, because the ground pressure tends to break and crack glass pieces when they are excavated. There are only two or three glass pieces out of a hundred that are found in this condition.

I knew I had to control my excitement so that I could make a good bargain. Merhdad pulled out a cigarette from his jacket and gave Ahmad one, and then both of them eagerly lit up. He kind of moved Ahmad's cigarette in front of my face so that I would notice. That was a brilliant move on his part and one I didn't expect. Merhdad was more cunning than I initially gave him credit for and he continued to surprise me.

I said, "Merhdad, can you please go out to the car and get our bags?" Merhdad was back in a flash with our luggage and I moved over to open my backpack that had the cartons of cigarettes. I pulled out three cartons and put them on the table in front of Ahmad.

He picked up one carton, turning it over and over and said, "*Marlboro*, good!"

I pointed to all three cartons and pointed at the glass vessel. He understood and raised his hand indicating five fingers. I put both hands up in the air showing him the inside of my palms. I then moved over to my bag and pulled out two more cartons, adding to the pile that now had five cartons. I said, "OK?"

He reached over with a big green toothy smile and shook my hand saying, "OK. OK." I had just made a deal for five cartons of cigarettes! I was happy and he was happy. It was a good deal for both parties, but little did I know that I had overpaid.

Merhdad then leaned over and said in my ear, "Two cartons OK."

"That's OK, I am happy. This is my first deal here. I want to make Ahmad my friend," I replied.

I then reached over and shook his hand again and said with a smile, "Good deal, you good friend." Ahmad smiled back and he was genuinely happy. I couldn't believe that I just did that deal for five cartons of cigarettes! As long as Ahmad was happy, everything was OK and we would not have any problems with him. It was important that he was happy, as he would watch our car when we were over the border. I began to think that I was glad that I wasn't hard on him with the deal. We had to have someone that could protect our backside when we were gone. There was no need to bargain with him; it was already a deal that was beyond good. We then settled down for some hot tea that was generously laced with honey and talked long into the night about that faraway fantasyland that was America.

CHAPTER THREE

The Armlets of Power

I awoke on a bed of wool Persian carpets that provided a firm, but comfortable sleep. I had slept like a baby and actually felt more rested than I had when I stayed at the hotel. Perhaps it was that strong tea with honey that I drank the night before, or perhaps it was the cool mountain air that made me sleep so well. Ahmad and Joni had a comfortable home, but then I thought the winters here would be extremely hard and relying on that fireplace for heat everyday would not be fun. I was the last to get up and around. Ahmad and Joni were up with first light and Joni had just finished the laundry down at the stream that ran behind the house. Ahmad had to go into Peshawar to do some business and would not return until nightfall. I walked outside to find Merhdad packing his bag with food and his camping gear.

"Kevin, we leave soon, OK? Sleep well?" Merhdad asked.

"Yes, and I am ready to go whenever you are ready," I said. He nodded in approval and then moved the car closer to the house against one of the walls and locked it up. Moving back into the house, we found Joni finishing up with her morning chores.

"Joni, your house is good and I slept well. See you in a few days," I said. Merhdad translated for me and she gave me a big smile. She said a few words to Merhdad and he said to me, "Joni say you good man. Come back, OK. See you soon."

I shook her hand and waved farewell. We both turned and made our way back out the door. I was thinking that I hoped to walk back through this door again. I was about to take the plunge into Afghanistan. I must be crazy to even think of a trip like this, but for some reason I felt that the trip would go smooth with no problems. Merhdad had made this trip several times with his cooking fuel and he knew exactly where we were going. As long as we did not stay too long, I felt that this hike would be worth the exercise.

We made our way down to the small creek that ran behind the house; its sandy bottom made for easy travel along the edge of the stream, rather than in the surrounding rocky terrain. "We follow stream up into mountains. Camp at border and sleep. Tomorrow we go into market. OK?" Merhdad said. I thought this was a good plan to camp on this side of the border and make a quick entry into the market the following day. This would cut our exposure in Afghanistan and give me a full day to see what was there.

"Lets camp on this side of border, OK?" I said.

Merhdad nodding in approval said, "Always do this, better. No worry about Russians. Good place to camp. No worry."

I looked at him and shook my head in agreement. Merhdad was not much of a man for words. He seldom talked except when he was addressed in conversation. He seemed to be in a rhythm with his walking in the creek bed. He moved steadily and with purpose, always scanning where he was walking. I followed his path as close as possible. The foothills ran higher and higher as we traveled and the wall of mountains rose up behind them like a curtain with a small opening where the stream ran through. That faraway gap in the mountain chain was our destination. The creek began to wind more like the body of a snake crawling over a flat surface. The foothills around the creek had small structures on top here and there, but there was nothing about them that looked like they were permanently inhabitable. Most of these buildings were in various stages of decay. I wondered how old some of these dilapidated brick walls were and my curiosity got the best of me.

"Merhdad, do people live there in those old places?" I asked. Merhdad looking at me with a slight grin replied, "No. Water hard to get up there. Some mujahideen camp there. Some live there. Not many live there."

I thought, not many people lived up there, but those old buildings could be far older than most people realized and perhaps were densely inhabited in antiquity. Mud brick structures such as these, that were high up from the streambed, were built first for defense then ease of living second. Carrying water up from the stream would be a secondary consideration in antiquity. Perhaps this was Pakistan's version of a cliff dwelling like Mesa Verde.

Bringing my eyes back down into the stream, I saw something at the edge of the sand where the stream had washed away a great deal of soil from the bank. My eyes were still sharp for searching the ground for objects. When my father and I used to hunt for arrowheads in Kansas when I was a kid, he taught me to scan the ground and look for things that were of a different color, a different shape, and looked unusual or out of place from the surrounding area. Walking over to the dark thing that caught my eye against the coarse gray white granular sand, I reached down to find a bronze javelin spear point that was about six and half inches long. The piece had an encrusted dark brown patina and sand began to fall out of the round shank at the end. I couldn't believe it. The piece looked to be early Roman, perhaps A.D. first to second century. The blades were not very rough at the edges and it looked to be in excellent condition, considering that the material was iron rather than bronze. An arid environment and a soil that is not heavily mineralized would aid in its preservation. The dry soil conditions here were perfect for an object such as this to survive in this mint state, and this would also explain why the glass piece survived as well as it did.

Another thought came to mind and the sand from both pieces had the same type of composition. It was probable that the glass vessel was found in another creek bed such as this, if not this same stream. It might pay to keep looking here after the rainy season, and based on my observations of erosion that could be seen everywhere, I was sure the creek bottom would get flushed every year with rushing water and everything would get moved around.

Merhdad came over to take a closer look and he whistled. I handled the object to him and he looked at it from all angles.

"Have you seen many more of these?" I asked.

"Yes, many. This one good. Maybe we see more," he said.

Merhdad patted me on the back and said, "We have more hours to go. You OK?" he said.

"Yes, my friend, no problem. I will follow you and happy to be here. I will stay behind you." I slipped off my backpack and placed the spear point inside and offered Merhdad some water.

"Few hours to camp. We rest there and make fire to cook. Have some fuel. Make tea," he said.

"Great. Let's get a move on," I said, as I patted him on the back and we began our trek up the stream.

The light was beginning to fade and the shadows were getting long after a few hours of walking. The mountains were really close and they just seemed to take off right out of the ground; it was if I could reach out and touch them. Their brown bases had sparse scrub grass here and there, then that gave way to massive slabs of rock that pointed almost straight up; their tops surmounted with a dusting of white blankets of snow that could be seen stretching down the rows of mountain peaks for as far as the eye could see. So this was the Hindu Kush. I had only one thought for this place and only one word came to mind—magnificent. The Alps and the Rocky Mountains were of no comparison. This mountain range was by far the toughest in the world. There were boulders in the foothills that were as large as a house and clouds always circled many of the peaks as if they had their own ecosystem. I thought it would be interesting to know if many of these peaks had ever been climbed.

I also recalled that at this point during the conquest of Asia by the Hellenistic Greek armies, the glory and riches of the conquest did not matter, but what really mattered was that they were in the pursuit of the gods. The Greek god Dionysus was thought to have reached India on his world crusade where he spread the gift of wine among mortals. A daughter of Helios, Circe, was thought to have told Odysseus that the afterworld lies at the extremity of the earth, beyond the vast ocean that encircles the flat known earth. This India for the ancients was, without doubt, the far extremity of the earth and within reach of the gods. This was an unknown world and for them, the end of the world was very near. For me too, this was an alien and faraway land and I was certain that I knew the feeling that they felt. This feeling of antiquity and this connection with the past, regardless of whether or not I was able to find any more objects, made this whole trip worthwhile. I realized at that moment, on the Afghan border, that it was the hunt for the objects, along with the enjoyment of finding and handling the objects, that I enjoyed the most. The thrill of unlocking the past through the objects began to appeal to me and not only did I find that each object had its own *raison d'être*, but the objects seemed to tell me much about their own history and degree of art.

The objects can speak to those who really begin to understand them and archaeologists to some degree understand this, but they are primarily concerned with what the object can tell them relative to its dating, its manufacture, and the more technical aspects of the piece as to how it might fit into the context of a dig. This is also why many archaeologists refer to objects as *artifacts*, rather than as *antiquities*. The beauty and the degree of art inherent with the piece, but more importantly, the artistic style and skill of the artist is perhaps something that most of them fail to see, and through this, there lies the true value of the object. Many professional dealers of antiquities have stated that most archaeologists see objects primarily as transmitters of knowledge, rather than as true works of art. I think this is the stance that most archaeologists have to take both politically and publicly, but in reality, I think that most of them appreciate the objects as works of art and are probably closet collectors.

The light was almost completely gone and at this stage of our trek, we had arrived at the gap that ran between two large mountain peaks. This gap was a saddle that was about one hundred meters wide. The stream had dropped off into a trickle and I knew that this had to be the border. Merhdad reached down and picked up a couple of large stones and moved over to the north side of the saddle, and there-against the face of a cliff-was a small rock shelter. Coming up to the shelter, I could see that there was a stonewall that protected a four-by-four-meter hollow in the cliff face. This petite shelter provided protection from the wind and upon closer inspection, the stonewall was built very well with large and small stones that interlocked with one another. Merhdad placed the two stones on top of the lowest section of the wall.

"Merhdad, did you build this?" I asked.

"Yes, Kevin. I put stone here. Then I come again and put stone there. Others that come, put stone there," he said.

"So, everyone that comes here puts a stone here?" I asked.

"Yes. Wall becomes big in short time. Mujahideen make these everywhere. This place not used much. More travel south over mountains," he said.

I looked at the care with which the wall was built and I thought that this was a group effort by people that probably didn't even know each other. If the mujahideen were doing this all over Afghanistan, then the Russians were sure to lose this war. Individual people working together like this are always stronger as a whole. Given modern weapons and this kind of determination, the Russians would all eventually end up going home in body bags. I doubted very much that the Russians were as organized as the mujahideen. The manner in which the Russian army was deployed in Afghanistan, mostly entrenched in the larger cities, made it impossible for them to build a structure such as this in the method in which it was done. Their units were not coordinated well enough to conduct joint military operations, which could carry the war effectively into the rural areas of the country. The mujahideen were able to move freely at night and strike anywhere at will. Perhaps I was reading too much into the wall, but one thing is certain and history always seems to repeat itself, and that is, *this part of the world was never really conquered.* The Hellenistic Greek armies controlled this region only because they allowed the local population to become part of the ruling elite and become an extension of their army. History was on the side of the mujahideen and nothing short of a nuclear blast could stop the onslaught. I felt sorry for the Russians, and I knew then there would be many more weeping mothers in Russia in the future.

We settled down for the night into the shelter; the cool air in the high mountain pass began to bite down into my body. I threw a thin gray cotton cape over my body that Merhdad had given me so that I could at least have some comfort for the night. I now realized why the mujahideen always wore these, and it was in part to keep them warm at night, but the real reason was so that they could not be seen. With the cape over their bodies in a crouching position, they would resemble rocks and would blend in with the rough terrain. Russian helicopters would often fly overhead and see nothing but inanimate objects. A simple cape such as this became their most effective piece of equipment.

Merhdad fired up his portable stove and began to heat some water for some hot tea. I tossed a few old empty bean cans into the fire pit that was at the end of the inside part of the wall, its thick, heavy blackened stones revealing many a visitor to this place. Islamic carving had been done on several faces of the stones and Merhdad explained they were prayers to protect the faithful from the sins of the earth. The shelter had enough room for at least four people and there was plenty of room for our blankets. I kicked off my boots and got under my cape; the cold was really starting to work its way under my skin.

"Here, Kevin. Tea finished," said Merhdad as he handed me a cup of the steamy tea. The tea was a welcome relief and I sipped it to warm my body core; it began to warm my insides and its comforting heat was a rare luxury in this part of the world.

"Will we go down to the market in the morning or wait till tomorrow afternoon?" I asked.

"We go in morning. Get there late afternoon. Market start in late afternoon, early evening. No problem with Russians. Hard to see us in late afternoon. Market time short, then we come back here tomorrow night. OK?"

I replied, "OK. Merhdad, no problem. I am ready to get in a lot of walking tomorrow. Let's get in and out fast, OK? Any sign of trouble, we punt and come back here fast, OK?"

"OK, Kevin. We get some sleep. See you tomorrow. Kevin, what is this punt?" he asked.

"Well, Merhdad, it means when things are not going so well, you punt. We cut our losses and move on. What can I say, I like the NFL. I'll try to explain this word more to you tomorrow. Good night."

"Good night, Kevin," he said.

I then drifted off to sleep, the biting cold making me even more tired. I thought that I had to be crazy to attempt a stunt like this, but then I thought this would be a once in a lifetime adventure. My last thought was keep your eyes open at all times and always be frosty. That night, I had some really bizarre dreams. There was this beautiful half-naked woman with open arms that was calling out to me from a distance, her open blouse blowing in the wind exposing her beautiful breasts; she kept calling to me to come to her. I was frozen and could not move towards her. I tried and tried to move closer to her, but I could not move. I then awoke with a start with Merhdad shaking my shoulder.

"Kevin. Get up. Get up. We go soon," Merhdad said. I

rubbed my face tying to get the blood to circulate more into my head. I felt like Rumplestiltskin awaking from a long sleep. What a dream! Shit. That woman, what the hell was that? I tried to recall her face, but that was useless. I began to move around and Merhdad handed me another cup of that hot tea.

"Thank you, Merhdad. Give me a few minutes to get my act together," I said with a yawn.

"Kevin. We go when you ready. Take time," he said with his familiar grin.

"Merhdad, I had this dream of this woman calling out to me and I could not reach her. What do you think it means? I have never had this dream. Do you think this is a warning? What do you think?" I asked.

"Kevin. No warning. I hear of dream before. I think this place calls to you. Good sign. Good sign," he said.

"Good sign, huh? OK, I believe what you say. Let's get down there and do our thing and get back, OK?" I then raised my hand and slapped Merhdad's hand and gave him a high five.

"OK! Let's go there!" he exclaimed.

Our breakfast was some fruit in a can, a slice of bread, a chocolate bar, and some water to wash it down. I felt good and well rested. That woman in my dreams didn't keep me awake so maybe she was a good spirit after all. I did some stretching, washed up a little bit, did my morning constitution, and I was ready to go. I now put my game face on and I remembered my college football days at the University of Colorado. I was still a Golden Buffalo fan and watched their collage games on TV every chance I got. I thought, well maybe this year they might have a decent team. I yelled at Merhdad, "Hey, I'm all suited up. Let's go kick some ass!"

Merhdad turned back to look at me and gave me the thumbs up signal. I suddenly felt better about the trip and I knew we would return here in one piece. Leaving the cooking gear and our blankets behind some rocks near the shelter, we packed up the rest of our gear and began to weave our way down the trail down off the saddle. The backside of the pass was strewn with rocks of all shapes and sizes. The trail started to become rough going and we had to work our way around many obstacles including some sharp gullies, loose gravel, and small holes in the path that could turn an ankle. We took our time and moved down off the part of the mountain that had the steepest angle, but the most dangerous part of the hike was yet to come.

After a few hours, we came up to a wide-open area that had absolutely no vegetation or any of the familiar scrub bushes that we could hide under. This area was the remains of an ice glacier that eons ago had left a field of broken rocks that were compressed into a tight compacted formation. We would literally have to walk from rock to rock in order to get through. This area fanned out from the higher elevations and got wider as it moved down slope. We would have to cross at a point that was near the top that was about a half mile wide. This wasn't far, but we were exposed on the open rock face and would become easy targets. It was still early in the morning and the sun was getting brighter and brighter, exposing the shadows that obscured our path that we intended to traverse. With each minute, our route was becoming more and more exposed, as the monochrome colors that were a constant in this part of the world were moving from black to gray.

"Merhdad, let's get across this fast. OK? I said. Merhdad nodded at me with approval and I knew he was thinking the same thing.

I then asked, "Do you always cross here this time of day?"

"Yes, Kevin. Never see anyone. Cross in ten minutes. Then move down next to cliff in dark," he said.

"OK, let's go for it, but first let's take a moment to secure our gear and listen for any choppers or anyone talking," I replied. We then knelt down and secured our backpacks for one another. I was glad we left the cooking gear and our blankets back at the shelter. The hike would be a lot easier. The clear mountain air could carry sounds for miles and there was nothing to hear except for the slight breeze that was blowing up from the valley below. This was the moment of truth, once we got by the open rock field, the rest of the way was easy going and there were many places to hide if we had to. I was glad Merhdad explained the route to me back at Ahmad's house.

Merhdad looked back at me and whispered, "Follow me close. I know way good and best rocks to walk. Do not talk for rest of way. We go quick, OK?" he said.

"OK, Merhdad. I am behind you." Merhdad then started out and I was behind him in a flash. He was sure of his footing and was aiming for a point that was slightly higher than we started from. I then could see why he was moving up and that was because the rocks we somewhat larger and we could then move very quickly from rock to rock. I moved at a rapid pace and did not look up, praying there would be no Russian choppers that would bear down on us or snipers hidden in the shadows to blow my head off. I kept looking down at the path and kept looking at the rocks, moving and moving, not stopping to rest and only looking up to see how far our objective was on the other side. I quickly glanced at my watch and we were about ten minutes into our sprint and then I looked once again at our objective and we were only about one hundred feet away. My lungs were heaving from the altitude. I was now twenty-eight years old and in excellent condition, but this sprint across the rocks really took it out of me. Merhdad was moving well ahead of me and I started to push it as hard as I could. It was like a tire drill that I was running through. My legs got heavier and heavier. Finally, we both hit the cliff face on the other side in about thirteen minutes and it seemed an eternity. The cool shade welcomed us both and we collapsed with heavy breathing. The cool mountain air was refreshing and I recovered very quickly. I patted Merhdad on the back and we began to make our way down into the shadows of the valley below. I could see there were some small settlements in the distance, but it was hard to make anything out this far away. I now felt safe and secure and there were a lot of large rocks about and there was plenty of cover for us. We also had a good view of the valley below.

Suddenly, we could hear the distant thump, thump, thump of chopper blades cutting through the thin mountain air. We both ran up behind some boulders and stayed down close to some big rocks that were the size of a small car. We pulled off our backpacks and threw them under a few rocks that had come together. We fell on our packs and then pulled ourselves up to scan the valley below and there, about five miles down the valley, three Russian choppers were making their way across the valley and were moving west by northwest into the next valley. I could clearly see a large red star painted on their rotor tails; it was truly the color of blood.

"Kevin. They go to Kabul. I see them sometimes. Never see them here. Nothing here. Mujahideen close to Kabul," Merhdad said, as he pointed at the choppers. I viewed the choppers and looked for the slightest turn if they made one. They kept their course and moved away. In a few minutes, there was total silence again. The choppers had left as quickly as they had come. I felt a little uneasy about this, but I was also glad to see them because I was now familiar with their sound and I felt I could gauge how far away they would be if I heard them again. We gathered our gear and slowly made our way down into the valley floor. I also took note that Merhdad had removed his weapon from his pack and placed it back after the choppers faded from view.

We came upon a group of five mujahideen that were relaxing under a large boulder. They were all armed and seemed very surprised to see us. The route down into the valley that we had taken was not one of the more popular ones, as the descent was tough going. Merhdad waved to them and I followed. They were shocked to see me and they all jumped up and started yelling, "CIA! CIA! CIA!"

I then said, "No CIA, I am tourist. I come to trade. Here catch!" They all lined up and I threw them each a pack of cigarettes. They were all smiles. Merhdad explained to them we were on our way to the market to look for a few souvenirs. They had a heavy weapon that looked to be an antiaircraft gun. The shells were about four inches long and they had boxes of ammunition. Merhdad explained to me they were ordered by Ahmad Shah Maksood to set up a mountaintop emplacement on the other side of the valley so to give the choppers a nasty surprise. They were constantly on the move and this weapon was always set up in a different position after they had made contact with the enemy. The Russians would come back after an ambush and as always there would be nothing to find. This war was a game of cat and mouse and who could hit who the hardest.

I was to learn later that this weapon was the feared DShK 12.7-mm antiaircraft machine gun which was capable of firing 575 rounds per minute. They said they had shot down two choppers in the last few months and they picked their spots well, so they could fire down on the choppers into the rotor blades and the top part of the aircraft that had no armor plating. Once the mujahideen were able to later obtain the shoulder-launched Stinger missiles in 1986, they were able to down about one chopper per day, and on September 26, 1986, they were able to down three choppers in one day near Jalalabad. This weapon could hit targets at altitudes up to 12,000 feet from the point of launch. From 1986 to 1987, about 900 Stingers were offered to the mujahideen and by the end of the war they were able to bring down about 269 aircraft and helicopters. Unfortunately, years later, many of these Stingers passed on to the Taliban, as evidenced by journalist Peter Bergen, who in December of 1999, saw Taliban soldiers carrying two Stinger missiles at the Kandahar airport. (See *Holy War, Inc.* by Peter Bergen, p.76.)

CIA advisors, organized by Milt Bearden, were training men and other commanders like Maksood inside Afghanistan. The US now had its proxy war against what Ronald Reagan coined "the evil empire" and it was a war that the Russians could never recover from, and the cracks in the empire began to grow larger and larger, as more and more body bags began to pile up day after day. There was little Russia could do to stop the bleeding, and she had become desperate, like a wounded animal that was running through the forest, leaving a blood trail that the hunters could easily follow, and would eventually fall to the arrows of the hunters. The ancient world had come home to the Red Army, for it was a total war to the death, and like the arena, there could only be one winner.

The deadliest arrow of them all was Maksood, who broke his forces up into these teams that were mobile and in the end, could wear down the Russian air force. It was Maksood who first developed this strategy of attacking the air mobility of the Russian air force and in reality, it was Bearden and the CIA who had much to learn from Maksood. Merhdad said a mobile force under Maksood's command spent three days hiding in the sand and got close enough to execute a massive mortar attack on the main airport at Kabul. The attack was at night and the morning revealed two hundred Russian dead and twelve aircraft destroyed. They retreated in teams and only a few of them were killed. There were other teams that were set up to ambush the Russians, as they were in pursuit and this blunted their retaliation. This victory was a big turning point in the war and it demonstrated to the rest of the mujahideen that Maksood was their best commander. In 1981, it was said the Russians had a five-million-dollar bounty on his head, dead or alive. The Russians later solved their problem with Maksood as they negotiated a cease-fire with him that lasted until April of 1984.

Maksood wanted the cease-fire so that he could take advantage of the precious stones at the mines of Dara-e-Khan that he recently captured and controlled. According to the Associated Press (September 10, 1982), Radio Free Afghanistan, Maksood was reportedly able to squeeze from the mines at Dara-e-Khan nearly one hundred million dollars per year. This was probably an exaggerated figure, but what stones he did sell were brought to London and then was sold into the international market. Naturally, fantastic antiquities started to show up as well. I thought that it was now a good time to be here, but unfortunately the cease-fire was now over and I had to be very careful. The entire region had become hot again and anything could quickly develop here.

My first meeting with these mujahideen went over well and we wished them farewell. By giving each of them a pack of cigarettes, not only went far in earning their trust, but also gave me an added feeling of security. I then began to wonder how many of them might be alive by the end of the year. We continued to walk for about another hour and I could see we were coming up on a group of mud brick houses that were spread along the sandy creek bank at the bottom of this valley that was nothing but endless sand and stone. There were several men, women, and children moving about and they appeared to be buying bread from a makeshift stand. Everyone was staring at me and I waved and smiled, several children came up and began tugging at my jacket. An elderly man appeared and Merhdad did all the talking and we followed him into a house that had no roof. The mud brick house had only three complete walls, but it was a shelter in which I could view some objects in a semi-private fashion. Merhdad had the old man scout around and we both stayed in the house. The old man quickly came back with a leather bag and he dumped the contents onto the ground before us. Both of them sat on the ground with us and we began to barter. The old man introduced himself as Abdul and the younger man, Hizbi, turned out to be his son.

There, on the ground before me was an ancient Greek Hellenistic silver cup, five cylinder seals, eleven silver tetradrachms of Seleukos I, two matching upper arm bronze armlets, and an assortment of bronze spear points. I asked how much for the whole lot. The son whispered into the old man's ear and he said five hundred dollars. Now that the mujahideen learned that these old items had value, they were no longer melting the coins down and were keeping a sharp eye at the ground. I reached into my backpack, careful not to reveal how much cash I had, and counted out the money before them. I also gave them a carton of cigarettes as a bonus. They were all smiles at this point and I was suddenly a hero. American cigarettes were the ultimate luxury item, as well as a status symbol. The son then pulled out another object from his robes. This piece was a leaping bronze lion that was the handle of a bronze vessel. It was approximately five inches long and it was in superb condition. I then pulled out five cartons and their eyes bugged out. The old man shook my hand and rattled off something to Merhdad.

"He says good deal. Good deal. He has more to show you," Merhdad said.

I looked at my watch and I said, "Merhdad I think we should now go. Have him save everything for your next trip here if he wants another deal. I would feel better not to stick around. Please carry all the pieces for me in your backpack and back to the shelter," I said. I thought that if some mujahideen should stop us on the way back, they would hassle Merhdad the least and there would be less risk for me in losing my pieces.

"No problem, Kevin. We go now," he replied. We got up and said good-bye to our newfound friends and we made our way out of the small village, with the children once again tugging at my jacket as we walked along. The old man yelled at them and they went running away laughing. I wondered if they were aware that there was a war going on here in their country. Merhdad gave the old man some final words about a possible future deal and then we all shook hands. That deal was a great deal, but I wanted to get back as soon as we could, now that I had a deal in my hands. Merhdad understood my urgency and we walked quickly and retraced our steps. In a few hours, we made it to the place where we ran into the five mujahideen, but they had moved on. In another hour, we had made it up into the open rock area and the light had faded and shadows from the mountain began to obscure the area we had to walk over. It was good timing, as the shadows would hide our walk over the rocks. This time there would be no sprint and we had to be careful to see where we were stepping. I did not want to turn an ankle at this point, with the climb up the mountain that was ahead. We quickly made our way over those damn rocks and we worked our way up the hill to the saddle, without speaking and stopping to rest. It took another hour to get to the safety of the saddle and the rock shelter. By now, it was dark and I never felt so much relief then to see that little rock shelter. I was pleased; the trip paid off and it went without a hitch. We retired to the rock shelter for a meal of rice and beans, and needless to say, I gobbled it all down in a few minutes. I was asleep minutes later and was out like a light.

The next day I awoke and it was midmorning. Merhdad was up and about as usual and he was making tea. "You sleep good. Have some tea and we go back if you wish," he said.

"Thank you for letting me sleep, Merhdad. Good of you to do so," I said.

Once again I got myself up and moving and we both walked out into the front of the shelter. I then spread the objects out that I purchased from Abdul and Hizbi. The Greek Hellenistic silver cup and the eleven silver tetradrachms represented the value of the deal. The cup was interesting and it was of the type that was illustrated in D.E. Strong's *Greek and Roman Gold and Silver Plate*, London, 1966, and was classified as late Hellenistic. The vessel had a hemispherical body and a concave upper part with a flaring rim. There was no design work and the vessel had a plain surface with a nice dark brown to black patina. This type derived itself from the earlier Achaemenid types that had elaborate fluting, ribbing, and leaf ornament on the lower body. Although this piece was plain with no decoration, it was still a rare and valuable piece.

The coins were of the type with the helmeted head of Seleukos I on the obverse and standing Nike goddess that was crowning a Greek victory trophy on the reverse. The conditions of these pieces were very fine to extremely fine. One particular coin that was of very fine condition had two letters of Aramaic script, on the reverse, seen below the standing Nike and the trophy. This, however, could be a control mark for the Susa mint, but it is significant in that the control mark looked to be Aramaic lettering.

A few years later, I was able to obtain another coin that was in mint state quality with this identical reverse die and these two pieces are probably the only two known examples. I sent a photo of this coin to Author Houghton who published *Coins of the Seleucid Empire from the Collection of Arthur Houghton,* the American Numismatic Society, New York, 1983.

Houghton agreed with me that this was extremely rare for a Greek coin to have this legend, as a coin like this legitimized Seleukos's rule as heir to Alexander the Great, and this type of legend probably was an indication that Seleukos I had local Persians in high political office that were key with the administration of his empire. This coin is perhaps the only proof that academics have relative to this theory.

The obverse was also significant, in that the portrait of Seleukos I bore an uncanny resemblance to Alexander's portrait seen on many of his earlier tetradrachms and other ancient works of art. However, this portrait may actually represent the portrait of Alexander the Great that assimilates the portrait of Seleukos himself and the portrait seen on this issue could pass for both rulers. This duality of portraiture would tie Seleukos closer to the divine status of Alexander, and as propaganda, was a brilliant stoke by Seleukos to help solidify his rule over the former eastern empire of Alexander. This not only tied him closer to Alexander, but also to the gods, as by the time Seleukos minted this issue a full twenty years after the death of Alexander, Alexander was considered a god. This issue may also have symbolized military victory of Seleukos over Chandragupta in India in 304 B.C., and this would explain the military victory trophy seen on the reverse. This coin was very important academically and I was happy to perhaps have saved it from the blast furnace.

The two matching bronze armlets were heavy and had two bullheads that came together at the top. They were of the Iranian type, as was the leaping lion bronze handle, and were about 4.5 inches wide and .5 inches in diameter. The armlets had wear on the inside surfaces and were worn by a powerful warrior chief. This person was an important person, as bronze in this period was very valuable circa eighth-seventh century B.C. In fact, the reason bronze was considered a valuable commodity was that it could be melted down and made into weapons such as a short sword or a mace head. I was to learn later on that the people during this period regarded bronze even more valuable than gold or silver for this very reason.

Judging from the wear on the inner surfaces, as they were worn above the biceps, this person probably wore these for life and they conveyed an image of power and strength. The armlets also conveyed the belief that the wearer was in control of the animals shown on the terminal end of the armlets. In this case, it was the bulls and/or calves seen on the armlets, which in antiquity represented wealth. This human/animal connection ties in with the idea that man has to domesticate and/or control animals for wealth, and this ensures the survival of the tribe. This theory is known as the *Master of the Animals Theory*, which was prevalent in antiquity. This theory may also explain why these armlets and bracelets with the animal head terminals were popular throughout the ancient Near East, at least as early as the ninth century B.C. An early example can be seen on a relief from Nimrud, that depicts the *apkallu* or protective spirit who wears an armlet of this type on each arm. (See J.E. Curtis and J. Reade, *Art and Empire, Treasures from Assyria in the British Museum*, New York, 1995, no. 8.)

Years later, I consigned the pair to auction and they didn't sell, and looking back on things, I was glad to have them returned to me and their presence has been felt by me for many years. The raw energy that they command leaves me no doubt that whoever owned these armlets was a master of his own destiny, and not only was he strong enough to have lived and fought in this arid land, he was also a person who was highly skilled with the art of war. In antiquity this land had to be the toughest on earth, because in those days war was fought hand to hand, not at a distance with guns and bullets. In those days there could only be one way home, and that way was through victory in war, which also meant a victory of life over death.

The armlets made me realize that this land was still at war and only the methods have changed, and the people here are as tough now as they were then, and this ancient way of life is really what these pieces have conveyed to me over the years. Although I could realize more for the other objects, it was those armlets and what they represented that had a value far more infinite than the monetary value they could have brought—for they are power pieces that are symbolic for a land and a time that still can be seen in a modern world.

Packing everything up, we made our way back down to Ahmad's house and we were greeted with a warm greeting. I was pleased that Ahmad seemed to like me, although we had not done a cash deal. I decided that if we did another deal in the future, I would offer him cash for the objects. The thought ran through my mind that his house would be a good staging area for me to have other people bring objects and he would get then collect a commission, but I decided against this, as the current government of Pakistan was becoming unstable and I didn't want to risk any problems for him and his family. I decided that if I would ever return again, I would see him at that time, rather than at a time when he was able to gather things. In this fashion I could control the prices better, although it would be hit or miss for me. As it turned out, this would be the last trip for me to this part of the world. One thing led to another for me in other countries and I let my contacts here go by the wayside. Perhaps this was a mistake, but as I was soon to know in the future, there would be plenty of business for me in other places that were easier for me to get to and not nearly as dangerous.

Before we left Ahmad's house, I decided to give him a few hundred dollars and half of my remaining cigarettes. I gave the other half to Merhdad, along with a sealed envelope with his five hundred and another five hundred as a bonus. Their spirits were uplifted and the conversation drifted about the spirit world and my dream that I had the first night I spent in the rock shelter. Sitting around that solid wood plank table, Ahmad explained to me through Merhdad that for some strange reason, this dream is a common dream that many foreigners had when they first visited their country. In fact, he thought that this type of dream was common for centuries and that the woman was a mother goddess for the area. One thing is for certain, the woman seemed real and I later thought that perhaps the woman represented Asia, who was calling for me to return. Those few days in the mountains would always return to my memories. It was a plunge into antiquity that few Westerners would ever experience and even fewer could really feel. I had truly traveled near the end of the world and close to the unknown horizon. Regrettably, the dream never returned and I have not been back since.

CHAPTER FOUR

The Hoard of the Century

Steve Rubinger, the President of Numismatic Fine Arts, Inc., sat stony faced, although his elegant Hermes tie was not out of place. He sat off to the side of the podium where Robert J. Myers, the auctioneer, was conducting the March 10, 1988 Numismatic Fine Art Auction XX, which was being held at the Le Bel Age Hotel in West Hollywood, California. The audience included collectors and dealers from around the world and there were many familiar faces that those in the trade would recognize. The Buddha-like Bruce McNall, who was chairman of the board, was not seen at the front table with the other officers of the company. McNall had become a busy man with his acquisition of the L.A. Kings hockey team and running his own movie company, Gladden Entertainment Corporation.

I took my seat midway from the front of the room and I could see all the bidding action that might happen from any corner. I happened to consign for this auction a coin of incomparable beauty, a silver tetradrachm that was minted in Athens, circa 465 B.C. It was listed in the catalog as number 694 and the technical description read:

Shortly after c. 465/2 B.C., silver tetradrachm (17.11gm). Starr Group V B (c. 454-449 B.C.), close to 174. *Lovely style. Extremely fine.*

The added description, seen below the obverse and reverse photos and the technical data of the coin, read as follows:

The owls of most of Group V are decidedly stout, especially in Group V B. The criteria for distinguishing the various series are so subtle as to be elusive. For example, Starr cites four features of Group V B, Series (1), three of them variable; and the only consistent feature, an ogival eye, is manifestly not present on his 174. He (Chester Starr) interprets the variety in the dies of this phase of the coinage as evidence that proper controls had broken down under the pressure of recoining the Delian treasury after its transfer to Athens in 454 B.C. His chronology is now suspect, and we may attribute the phenomenon rather to artistic ferment and exploration.

In other words, my coin was a transitional piece that was minted between the archaic and classical periods of Greek art, and issues from this time frame are extremely rare. I expected the bidding to be strong and I waited for the fireworks to begin.

Once the auction began, I noticed a foreign-looking gentleman that was seated to my immediate right and he was following my viewing of the catalog. He had no catalog so I offered to share it with him during the sale. He seemed to be of Middle Eastern origin in his fifties, with glasses, thinning short dark hair, and slightly paunchy build. His English was good, but he had a Turkish accent. I thought nothing of this, as the room was full of people from all over the world.

He commented on this coin or that coin and asked, "That seems a lovely coin, is that the best grade that it can be found?" or he would comment, "Is that rare?"

Thinking he was a new collector to the market, I felt free to comment to him on the sale and certain coins that were illustrated in the catalog. Finally, the auction moved on to lot number 659 and the technical description read:

Thraco-Macedonian Tribes, Bisaltae, c.470-465 B.C., silver octodrachm, unpublished variety. Ex South Anatolia *(Decadrachm) hoard. 1984. Obverse slightly off center. Superb.*

The added description, seen below was very detailed and unusually lengthy, read as follows:

The Decadrachm hoard contains the most important body

of Bisaltae coinage ever discovered, or assembled. Full revelation must await publication of the hoard by J. Kagan and J. Spear. But certain preliminary findings have already been reported (S. Fried, "The Decadrachm hoard: an introduction," and J. Kagan, "The Decadrachm hoard: chronology and consequences," in Coinage and Administration in the Athenian and Persian Empires: The Ninth Oxford Symposium on Coinage and Monetary History, BAR International Series 343 (Oxford, 1987, p. 1f and pp. 22-25). In addition the cataloguer has benefited from the study of hoard photographs kindly made available to NFA.

Nearly thirty obverse dies are represented in the hoard, most of them new, and there is much die linkage within the series: apart from four singletons, the 68 octodrachms in the hoard can be organized into fourteen die-linked groups. All obverse dies are of the inscribed variety; only two previously known inscribed dies are not included in the hoard, and these can be identified as the latest in the series.

The hands of at least two die engravers can be recognized on the hoard's octodrachms. One worked in a rather idiosyncratic late archaic style that features strange deformations of the horse's open mouth (see Fried, art cit., Pl. I, 1-3). Apparently the mint's first engraver, he also executed the earlier uninscribed obverses not represented in the hoard. The other engraver, the author of the octodrachm offered here, created fresh and attractive dies in the transitional (or "severe") style. He engraved the two die varieties with a control symbol in the right field (the helmet, on the latest Bisaltae dies represented in the Decadrachm hoard, and the satyr head, on the next die of the series, not represented in the hoard). Besides the obverse die of this octodrachm, known from five examples, the engraver in question produced one other die bearing a different brand on the horse's flank (known from only two examples). It is possible that the horse on the die with the helmet symbol bears yet a third brand. These facts suggest that the octodrachm varieties with the brand immediately precede those with the control symbols, and indeed the brands may represent the first attempt to devise a control system.

The presence of so much Bisaltae silver in this hoard, in association with Athenian decadrachms and contemporary Athenian tetradrachms, confirms the suggestion of Price and Waggoner (Archaic Greek Silver Coins: The "Asyut" Hoard, London-Encino, 1975, p.39) that the coinage of the Bisaltae dates from "the time of the Athenian expedition to gain a foothold on the Thracian coast c. 475-465." Kagan hypothesizes that the Bisaltae won control of the silver mines around Lake Prasias upon Persian withdrawal, and that their coinage was terminated around the time of the foundation of the Athenian colony at Ennea Hodoi and the subsequent disaster at Drabescus, 465/4 B.C. This battle, in which the native Thracians exterminated the Athenian colonists, may have enabled Alexander I of Macedon to take possession of the mines for himself. The Bisaltae octodrachms, like other elements in the hoard, display little wear even on the earliest specimens and must have entered the hoard en bloc from the treasury of the Bisaltae, perhaps as tribute to Athens or the Delian League.

This description read like a book and was unusually long for a coin description that was in an auction of this type. NFA was known to comment on coinage that was unusual, rare, and/or had exceptional artistic style such as the coin that I consigned, but the descriptions for the coinage that originated from the *Decadrachm Hoard* was unusually long. In a way, that did not surprise me because everyone in the trade knew the hoard was one of, if not the most important, ancient coin hoards discovered in the last one hundred years or maybe in modern history.

This hoard contained mint state coinage that was assembled by Athens and her vassal states, probably as a military payroll, for the struggle against the Persians in Anatolia, which is in modern-day Turkey. The hoard contained a little over two thousand silver coins—a staggering amount, considering they were all mostly mint state quality. The hoard contained fourteen decadrachms that were minted by Athens and together with the specimens found in the hoard there are twenty-seven recorded pieces. The decadrachm was possibly a commemorative issue, and the reason for its creation is still being debated by numismatists, but my theory is that this issue was created as sort of an "*esprit de corps*" issue, which celebrated the recent military turn of the tide against the Persian Empire. Most numismatists have debated this event, or that event, as the motivation for the issue, but I think it was an accumulation of events that led up to the Persian military setbacks, circa 480-465 B.C., that resulted in its creation circa 470-465 B.C. The Athenian state needed an extra shot in the arm to help keep the momentum going and for the moment, the gods were on their side. There would be no better motivation for their military in the field than to have their soldier/citizens receive such a coin for exceptional courage and valor. After circa 480 B.C., it was actually considered vogue for her citizens to serve in the military. This coin represented the heart of the Athenian onslaught and her empire was now at her peak. Never again would Athens attain an empire that gave her dominance in the Mediterranean region, and never again would Athens attain the wealth and military strength that she now enjoyed.

Whatever the impetus for its creation, this coin is one of the most celebrated coins minted in antiquity, thus the name *Decadrachm Hoard* was a good description. The last specimen sold at public auction realized $300,000.00 in 1974 and it was in very fine condition. The value of the recently found pieces would be infinitely greater—they were all in mint state condition.

During the auction, the foreign gentleman blandly asked me a question that a neophyte collector might ask. "What was so special about this *Decadrachm Hoard?*"

I replied, "Because the bulk of the coinage is in mint state condition, there are excessive rarities, and never before has a wide variety of ancient coinage been found that is like this. In short, it is the hoard of the century, perhaps one of the greatest ancient numismatic coin hoards ever found."

With this answer, the foreign gentleman seemed to stiffen and he leaned over and said, "Good luck with your auction."

I thought his reaction to my answer was a bit strange, but then lot number 663 came up and I forgot about the man next to me who then slipped away during the sale. Lot number 663 was also from the *Decadrachm Hoard* and it was a silver tetradrachm from Acanthus, a brilliant coin that had a recumbent bull kneeling down on one forward leg with a lion on top that was biting down into his back. It was a powerful coin.

I had the high bid on the floor and I quickly found I was bidding against the book bids that the auctioneer had. I dropped out and the coin went to the book. I then thought that it was strange that the prior four lots, that were all listed from the *Decadrachm Hoard* and described as, "Ex South Anatolia *(Decadrachm) hoard,* 1984," all went to the book and were sold to an unknown bidder. Later in the sale, the other coins from the *Decadrachm Hoard* met the same fate. There was some murmuring in the room as lot after lot attributed to the *Decadrachm Hoard* went to the book. There were a total of ten coins that were "bought in" by NFA and the reason for this was clear; the coins were listed as being from South Anatolia, i.e., Turkey. NFA had set a precedent in actually listing the find spot for the coins, as most auction catalogs do not list such find spots simply because they might have been found in a wide variety of countries. However, the *Decadrachm Hoard* was an unusual circumstance because the hoard found its way to OKS Partners, Inc. in 1984 and bypassed the heavyweight players in the international market, namely NFA and Bank Leu of Zurich, Switzerland. OKS beat them to the punch and purchased the bulk of the hoard for $3.5 million, the hoard consisting of approximately 2000 coins that weighed about 58 pounds, the equivalent of one talent in antiquity.

A talent in the fifth century B.C. could buy 150 slaves and

four tetradrachms could buy a mercenary soldier for a month, the total paying 475 men for one month's service. In effect, one talent of silver could pay for a small army for a whole month, and Athens and the Delian League probably created the totality of the *Decadrachm Hoard* for this purpose. In antiquity, to have the money and an army for a month meant that you could go out and conquer the country of your choice. It also meant that you could gain that country's goods and services, which were worth tenfold, or maybe even more, depending upon how wealthy the land was and how long you could control the region. This scenario gives one the realization of exactly how important and massive this hoard was really worth in antiquity.

OKS stood for Oxbow Corp. owned by William I. Koch, the K for Jonathan H. Kagan, and the S for Jeffrey Spier. Koch was the moneyman of the partnership and his net worth at the time of their purchase was approximately $550 million, so his purchase of the hoard was an investment he could easily afford. The other two partners, Kagan and Spier, were both Ivy League graduates with an interest in ancient history. They convinced Koch to put up the bulk of the cash to buy the hoard and they would then embark on an academic crusade to publish and bring the hoard into the limelight; by doing so, they would then probably bring up the monetary value of the hoard. This can also explain the lengthy description of the *Decadrachm Hoard* coins in the NFA catalog that is seen above. It can also explain the thoughtful publications, which are also named above, that both Kagan and Spier brilliantly completed. Their organization of the symposium on the hoard at Oxford, England in 1987 was also commendable, in that several academics were able to present several papers relative to the hoard and this greatly expanded our knowledge of the coinage. Their plan to slowly release the coins into the market was going well and several sales had taken place, but the NFA catalog, with ten of their coins listed, suddenly showed up and it turned out to be a disaster.

The catalog attracted the attention of the Turkish government who could easily see that the coins were listed as coming from South Anatolia, i.e., Turkey. Ancient coins sold on the international market today are legally auctioned, because their find spots could be in any of several countries and in most cases, no one can prove exactly where and when they were originally excavated. The Turkish authorities demanded that the coins be returned to Turkey on the grounds that they were stolen cultural patrimony. For Turkey to make this claim, I wondered if they first considered their own history, vis-à-vis the past generations from Abdul Hamid to Ataturk that drove roughly three million Greeks and Armenians abroad. The coins listed in the NFA catalog and about half of the coins that comprised the entire hoard were originally minted in ancient cities that are outside of modern Turkey, so the first question that came to my mind was, whose cultural patrimony is being stolen anyway?

It is a known fact that Athens and the Delian League originally minted the bulk of the hoard to support their military in the field against the Persians and were the original owners of the hoard, and for Turkey to claim the coins as cultural patrimony, even though the coins were found within the modern state of Turkey, seemed rather ludicrous. Greece and Turkey were ancient enemies and are still not on the warmest of terms. The invasion of Cyprus by Turkey is still a sore issue between both nations and upon reflection, it seemed to me that Greece would have more of a legitimate claim for the coins, considering that the basis for the Turkish claim was their own cultural patrimony. Could it be that Greece did not file their own cultural patrimony claim for the coins because they did not want to be seen as inflaming the fragile international concord that now exists between both countries?

As far as I know, the government of Greece never considered filing a claim, or if they did, they never followed through and filed a claim in the United States or anywhere else. More likely, since the coins were found within Turkey, their legal case would be nullified, but considering Turkey's past history, a claim such as cultural patrimony might have been a plausible course of action for the Greek government to consider.

The question is, since Turkey probably had some sort of a claim to the coins because they were proven to have been found within Turkey, did Turkey have the right to claim them in the name of "cultural patrimony," given the facts of Turkey's past history and that the bulk of the hoard was minted in antiquity within the modern state of Greece by Athens and the members of her empire, the Delian League, and can Greece in turn file a claim against Turkey in the name of "cultural patrimony?"

In order to avoid any legal entanglements, NFA bought back the *Decadrachm Hoard* coins that were listed in their own auction and turned them over to the Turkish government without so much as a whimper. Bruce McNall either committed a huge screw-up with his own catalog, or more likely, he wanted to teach OKS a lesson, the lesson being stay out of our backyard and leave the market to the established players. McNall knew how to play hardball and his new game now was hockey, complete with the tough body checking. Steve Rubinger's stony expression during the sale now became more apparent to me and I was sure he did not like what was going on with the "buy-ins." It was bad business to have the few other bidders like myself squeezed out from acquiring any of the *Decadrachm Hoard* coins in the auction.

OKS now had a huge legal problem with the Turkish government and its lead lawyer, Lawrence M. Kaye, began to turn up the heat on OKS. Koch eventually solved his legal problems by announcing his returning of the *Decadrachm Hoard* to Turkey in an official ceremony held at the Turkish Embassy in March of 1999. Kenan Yurttagul, Acting Director General of the General Directorate of Monuments and Museums presented Mr. Koch with a medal, for relinquishing the estimated $10-million-dollar hoard. It is also probable that Mr. Koch collected a sizable U.S. tax deduction.

Bruce McNall, as of this writing, is now sadly trading cigarettes at the federal minimum-security prison in Boron, California, and is serving nearly a six-year term, which may be reduced in the near future for good behavior and McNall's apparent willingness to make amends for his transgressions. The front page of the *Los Angeles Times* dated January 10, 1997 read:

The criminal activity involved creating phony financial statements as far back as 1984, supplying fake inventories of valuable coins in order to secure loans, diverting money from King ticket proceeds and a Merrill Lynch coin fund (Athena Fund II). Even Gretzky was deceived as McNall and his associates improperly pledged a horse co-owned with Gretzky to a bank without telling the hockey player.

McNall had dug himself into a pit that was too deep for him to pull out. Numismatic Fine Arts and its ancient coin holdings enabled McNall to leverage real estate loans that he began to shuffle like a deck of cards. It was only a matter of time before the bank regulators began to zero in.

Steve Rubinger, the former President of NFA, still works in Los Angeles and runs his own company called Antiqua. He avoided the legal problems faced by McNall and left NFA before the problems started to get out of hand, and he probably saw the writing on the wall of what the future would unfold for both NFA and McNall. The high degree of academic scholarship seen in his catalogs is a reflection of his personal knowledge and he is a credit to the trade.

The foreign gentleman at the auction turned out to be none other than Ozgen Acar, who was a Turkish journalist that was clandestinely gathering information for his upcoming article that was published in the July, 1988 issue of *Connoisseur* magazine. The article was titled *The Hoard of the Century* and the cover of the magazine featured a drawing of an Athenian decadrachm. The editor-in-chief of this now defunct publication was Thomas Hoving, book author and former director of the Metropolitan Museum of Art in New York. His positions regarding the antiquities trade are well known among many dealers and collectors, especially in New York, and his publishing of Acar's article and probable association with Ozgen Acar did not surprise me.

Acar is well known in Turkey for his work published in the Istanbul daily newspaper, *Cumhuriyet*, and was known to have contributed and traded information with other journalists in other countries relative to the antiquities trade. He tends to get around and attended the Koch medal ceremony at the Turkish embassy in March of 1999 and has been seen with Kenan Yurttagul in New York on numerous other occasions. He has demonstrated, through his knowledge of the trade and his published articles, that he is sort of a point man on behalf of the government of Turkey. His articles seem to be a precursor for the Turkish government's "jihad" to recover objects that they brand as being cultural patrimony, and Acar's role in Turkey's recovery and return to Northern Cyprus of the *Kanakaria mosaics* is eerily familiar to the circumstances that surrounded the *Decadrachm Hoard*. Objects would be identified, articles published, arrests of suspects would be made and/or muscled, and then finally, legal counsel would enter the picture for possible recovery.

One of my clients, who is an avid collector and has a keen interest in Roman bronzes, works in Langley, Virginia. True to form, he was always vague as to what his true job description was. His take on Acar was that he was in fact on the Turkish government's payroll from time to time and his guise as a journalist was only a mask. He had the opinion that Acar was "active in New York City in gathering information relative to NATO and the U.S. military capabilities in Turkey." In addition, he felt Acar was "instrumental in passing information relative to the perceived U.S. assessment of the Kurdish problem that Turkey was having within its own borders."

Turkey is currently under the magnifying glass of several human rights groups including Human Rights Watch and Amnesty International. The Kurdish conflict within Turkey has led to much criticism of Turkey abroad, and has been cited as one of the main obstacles for Turkish membership into the European Union. Turkey now has a tremendous tourist industry that brings in millions of dollars per year and news of human rights abuses could damage Turkey's fun in the sun industry. My client further suggested that, "Acar is fine-tuned, relative to these issues, and provides damage control and propaganda in a journalistic capacity on behalf of the Turkish government."

My own research revealed that Acar was active in mid-1989 in producing several articles about Balkan smuggling routes and the looting of Byzantine antiquities in Turkey and the Turkish Republic of Northern Cyprus. These antiquities included mosaics, which are comprised of small-multicolored tessarre tiles and are, in many instances, mounted on walls and ceilings of Byzantine basilicas that date back to circa A.D. 500. They convey a powerful religious feeling when viewed in the dimly lit basilicas and often portray detailed facial features of Jesus and his Apostles. The timing of Acar's articles seen in *Cumhuriyet* coincided with the Turkish Republic of Northern Cyprus filing suit for a recovery action in federal court in Indianapolis in March 29, 1989, for the mosaics known as the *Kanakaria mosaics*.

In late May of 1989, the trial began and on August 3, a decision was ruled on by Judge Noland to return the mosaics to Cyprus from a woman named Peg Goldberg. It was Judge Noland's ruling that Goldberg failed to show that she had clear title for her four mosaics, as they were previously published and photographed in 1977 prior to her purchase. They were published in one of a series of monographs sponsored by the Dumbarton Oaks Center for Byzantine Studies in Washington, D.C. A.H.S. Megaw and E.J.W. Hawkins titled the volume, "The Church of the Panagia Kanakaria at Lythrankomi in Cyprus: Its Mosaics and Frescoes." Cyprus apparently had an open-and-shut case for their recovery because of the prior Dumbarton Oaks Center publication which positively identified the *Kanakaria mosaics* through matching photographs, and this tied them to their original location. Acar's articles really had no bearing on the outcome of the *Kanakaria mosaics* court case, but they seem to reveal a pattern that Acar was pursuing with his journalistic endeavors, and perhaps more revealing, his probable high level ties within the Turkish government.

The last glimpse I had of Ozgen Acar was in New York in September 1988, during the Greater New York Numismatic Convention at the Omni Park Central Hotel on 7th Avenue and 56th Street. I had set up a dealer display table at the convention and it was a four-day affair with most of the leading U.S. dealers of ancient coins in attendance. The director of the show was the personable Moe Weinschel, who had the typical New Yorker's accent and blue-collar mindset. He was a no-nonsense sort of fellow who ran a clean and organized event. The security by John C. Mandel Security Bureau was excellent and photo identification was required of all the dealers. All visitors into the show had to register and pay a nominal fee for the length of the event; there were no exceptions.

Into the second day of the show, Ozgen Acar showed up with a film crew. He began filming many of the various dealers and began moving the camera up close to view their inventories that were secured in glass cases. Several of the dealers began to complain about being filmed at the show, because they were concerned about their safety and did not want their inventory filmed. Acar was filming without their permission, which was in violation of the show's by-laws, and several customers there also voiced some concerns. Acar may not have been familiar with the show's by-laws and he may have correctly registered his film crew at the reception desk, but he absolutely had no permission to film individuals that were conducting business in the show that did not want to be filmed, nor did he have permission to film inventory without the owner's approval. His camera crew had swept about halfway through the show, up and down the rows of display tables, taking in as much as they could record, when Moe appeared with his security crew and asked him what he was doing. Acar did not have a satisfactory answer for him and he asked Acar to leave, along with his camera crew. Acar tried to slip out with the film in the camera, which looked to be a standard size TV shoulder camera with a huge light on top, but security had quickly detained him and had to physically remove the film from the camera with the advice of the FBI. Moe then promptly threw them out under the observation of the New York City Police Department.

There was speculation among several dealers, including Victor England and Ed Waddell, that Acar was attempting a "set up" and was engaging in cheap "ambush journalism." Other dealers were speculating that Acar was filming on behalf of a Turkish TV station, but whatever the reason, Acar was foiled in his attempt to blatantly film whoever and whatever moved in front of the lens. I learned later that Acar falsely represented to the show organizers that his Turkish film crew was from a local TV station, and that what interviews and footage he obtained from many of the dealers in attendance could have been for use on Turkish TV and perhaps, even for the Turkish government. I expected more from a professional journalist than a tawdry stunt such as this, but then again, the use of journalistic credentials as a cover is well known and used by most major governments.

This was the last time I saw Ozgen Acar, but he popped up again in early January of 1990, and his role this time was that of an informant. He informed the editorial staff of *Coin World*, a major weekly numismatic newspaper, that the Turkish government was suing Koch and several more Americans connected with the purchase of the *Decadrachm Hoard* for $30 million in damages. The suit, lodged in Massachusetts, was familiar to Acar as he was instrumental in providing *Coin World* with the actual legal papers. In fact, he arranged the legal documents to be faxed to *Coin World*, so that they could have them in time in order to break a major story. Dr. Arnold R. Saslow also confirmed this in an article titled "The Turkish Connection," that was published by *Minerva* magazine in March 1990.

The Numismatic Fine Art Auction XX in March 1998 turned out to be more than just an auction. It set into motion forces that began to attack the antiquities trade in the United States and wealthy collectors were now the targets. I had a ringside seat for what I believed was the beginning of an attack on collectors in the United States and Europe. I decided then to inform collectors as best I could about some of the politics relative to the market and explain to them the varied positions that people have towards the trade. My outlook towards the trade actually strengthened during this period in time, and I knew that deep inside the beauty and enjoyment of the objects was, and still is, what is really important for me. As time went by, I saw in many of the collectors that I had the pleasure to work with a mirror of myself, and it was this mirror that made it all worthwhile.

CHAPTER FIVE

Who's Who

The positions regarding the antiquities trade are varied and are diverse. As I noted earlier in this work, everyone has a different opinion regarding the trade and that opinion tends to be influenced as to how one fits into the scheme of things. There are now three basic camps, or groups of people, that have a distinct viewpoint and outlook about the inner workings of the trade. These camps have recently started to emerge and their positions are becoming more clear and defined. There are also many people that take a position of more than one camp and prefer a blend of perhaps all three. I will try to simplify these views and give you, the reader, a basic understanding of the views and opinions of these three groups.

The first camp that I would like to define is the group that I would like to call the *Universal Internationalists.* This group is mostly comprised of dealers, academics, museum curators, and collectors. This group follows the idea that art is a universal form of expression and that collectors have a right to freely collect antiquities in a free society.

Collector heavyweight George Ortiz perhaps summed up this train of thought the best; "The criticisms against antiquities collecting are an assault on the universality of liberal humanism and an attempt to define the self as something harmful to the general good. These critics are trying to kill the free circulation of cultural knowledge and plunge the world into nationalism and ethnocentricity." (See *Art & Auction*, February 15, 1999, from "The War on Collecting" by Steven Vincent, p. 35.)

A great many museum curators understand what Ortiz has to say, in that art is a great "icebreaker" and tends to break down cultural barriers between people, thus bringing the world closer together with greater understanding of perceptions, principles, and cultural values between nations. Museum curators promote the free exchange of objects between institutions and the international idea of *shared cultural heritage*. This concept of shared cultural heritage for the most part runs counter to the idea of cultural patrimony.

Cultural patrimony is a concept that is analogous as to how Americans might feel-for example, towards the Statue of Liberty. This object is ours; it belongs to no one but our nation; it is not for sale; it defines our national identity, and cannot leave the country; and in a nutshell, this analogy is the root basis concerning the concept of cultural patrimony. However, the true meaning of the term cultural patrimony is difficult to define, because the idea that modern nations entirely derive their modern culture from prior cultures is somewhat ambiguous, as we now live in a non-homogenous world that is multiethnic and is a mix of many cultures that are completely different from those cultures that dwelled in the past, and this would especially apply to those cultures that were extant in antiquity.

A great many art dealers that follow the Universal Internationalist view regard cultural patrimony as a pretext for many "art-rich" countries to nationalize objects of art. Recently, Turkey and Egypt have declared their ownership of certain objects in private collections within their borders, including those collections that have been extant for generations.

Arielle Kozloff, vice president of Ancient Art at the Merrin Gallery in New York has stated, "Cultural patrimony claims are part of a power struggle, a way for leaders to rouse anti-imperialist sentiments and unify their populations. The idea of cultural patrimony is more important to the leaders of these nations than any of the objects involved."

Sam Merrin, the son of Ed Merrin who owns the gallery, has brought up another point for the Universal Internationalist camp and he has stated, "These countries didn't begin to care about their objects until they took on a market value. This issue of cultural patrimony really hasn't entered the mainstream of discussion regarding the antiquities trade, until the market began to endow objects with a dollar value." (See *Art & Auction*, ibid above, p.38.)

My case in point is the coins that would have otherwise been melted down in Afghanistan, and because there was a perceived value for the coins, they were preserved and made their way into the market. The realization of a market with value has also spurred nations to protect and control their objects, and they have all embraced the concept of cultural patrimony by signing the UNESCO accords that were drafted in 1970, which controls the export of objects between countries.

The Universal Internationalists are also concerned about the radical degree that many nations have taken towards cultural patrimony. The Universal Internationalists think that these nations view the hundreds of duplicate pieces, that are stored in boxes and crates in the basements of their museums, as falling under the definition of cultural patrimony and have refused to do anything with them, including placing them on display or trading them with other institutions for objects in other countries. There have been many suggestions by those in the trade that these countries sell some of their duplicates and use the money to protect the sites that they have already excavated and begin to upgrade their decrepit museums. Many politicians and academics in the "art-rich" nations and most archaeologists worldwide have met this suggestion mostly with hostility.

Arielle Kozloff further explains why most nations have not sold any of their duplicate pieces, "The *idea* of cultural patrimony is more important to them than any of the objects involved. Officials have told me that the reason they retain the objects is for tourism. That's why they don't deaccession—antiquities comprise a huge economic machine." (See *Art & Auction*, ibid above, p. 38.)

John Henry Merryman, art law expert and professor emeritus at Stanford University Law School, is an academic that has also made this suggestion, but he points to another issue, and that issue deals with the export laws of the "art-rich" countries themselves. He believes that these laws are grossly archaic and constitute the core problem regarding large-scale looting in source countries. He has stated that the problem is not the trade, but rather one based simply on supply and demand. He blames the ridged export laws of "art-rich" countries and a constant stream of propaganda from the archaeologists for keeping the supply short and driving prices up. Once the prices escalate, so does the black market and the whole thing then becomes a vicious circle. He believes that the demand will always be there and there will always be people that will want to collect, no matter what laws are enacted or what anyone says.

Merryman also recently stated the following in the *New York Times*, Aug. 1, 2003, in an article titled "Ancient Art at Met Raises Ethical Questions" by Martin Gottlieb and Barry Meier:

"Museums and collectors play a vital role by preserving art that, while it may lack provenance, has been shielded from war, vandalism or neglect."

The museum that is the most outspoken relative to the issue of cultural patrimony and is perhaps the leader that best represents the Universal Internationalists mode of thinking is the British Museum. The issue of the Elgin Marbles is well publicized and the museum's recently appointed director, Neil MacGregor, clearly explains the museum's rejection of Greece's demand that the museum return the Elgin Marbles, which were brought in 1811 from the Parthenon in Athens by Lord Elgin, as a matter of principle, in that the British Museum was founded in 1753 as the world's first national museum that embraced a universal collection of the whole world under one roof. Neil MacGregor further explains this *universalist* viewpoint in the *New York Times* on June 24, 2003, in an article titled "British Museum, at 250, Heads to Calmer Waters" by Alan Riding:

"Why was Great Britain the first country to create a national museum? Because it was in harmony with free citizenship, religious tolerance, and the need for informed citizens. The Greek government has asked for their (Elgin Marbles) perpetual return, and on that basis the trustees of the museum cannot negotiate.

About 40 percent of the sculptures are lost forever. Of what survives, half is in Athens and roughly half is here. You can argue that works of art are best shown in their place of creation. But you can argue that they are best seen in the context of the great works of mankind. So the issue is whether you believe in a museum that pulls together the achievements of humanity as a whole. The eighteenth-century idea was that culture united people. That is relevant today. That's why you need a universal collection."

On the other end of the spectrum, are the **Ethnocentric Nationalists.** This group is comprised mostly of archaeologists, academics, and politicians. This group follows the concept that art should only be owned by the state, rather than the "individual," and they follow a retentive view that all "art-rich" countries have a right to retain all art that was, and is now, within the boundaries of the state. The basic concept of private property rights does not figure into their mode of thinking and the state should decide what should be done with the art and who should own and handle it. Archaeologists worldwide follow the theory that they are best qualified to handle objects and they alone are best suited to find, restore, and evaluate them. Politicians, who follow this concept of state ownership of art, generally support nationalistic policies in order to unify the populace and define an ethnocentric sphere of influence within their own borders. I think that the concept of cultural patrimony is in part, a byproduct of this corpus of thought.

Collectors like George Ortiz have also expanded on defining cultural patrimony by suggesting that it is a very broad term in our multicultural world today. The world today is not as homogeneous as it once was and Ortiz has stated in public many times, "There is no such thing as cultural patrimony, like there is no such thing as pure race!"

The corpus of the Ethnocentric Nationalist thinking is based on protectionism and one of their most outspoken adherents is Archaeological Institute of America (AIA) Vice President for Professional Responsibilities and Director of the Office of Public Archaeology at Boston University, Ricardo J. Elia, who has said, "The bottom has to be knocked out of the entire antiquities market. Collectors and dealers are like dinosaurs. They think it's still the eighteenth century, when you could rip things out of archaeological sites and put them on your mantel." (See *Art & Auction,* ibid above, p. 35.)

The governments of Egypt, Italy, Peru, and Turkey have gone as far to require their own citizens to register antiquities that, in some cases, have been in family collections for generations. They have recently declared that all antiquities are property of the state and that failure to properly register antiquities is grounds for seizure. Of course, if an object is a very important piece, the owner still runs the risk of the piece being seized even after it has been registered, as these owners often do not have adequate documentation that proves that they have owned their pieces for a significant amount of time.

The concept that private property may be seized due to the reasons noted above, runs counter to our western idea of English common property law and the private property rights of individuals in a free society. The laws created by the "art-rich" countries are clearly protectionist in a realistic sense and fit well with the concept of cultural patrimony. It can be said that the heart of the Ethnocentric Nationalist line of thought lies with the governments and the laws of the "art-rich" countries themselves.

The group that is in the middle of the spectrum is the **Centralists.** This group is comprised of people from both ends of the spectrum that follow the idea that culture does figure into the equation as to who should and can own art, i.e., the state, or the "individual," or perhaps both, and that the rights of the private owner should be fully respected and recognized. The Centralists are by in large "pro" market and think that the antiquities trade can have a productive and useful future in bringing duplicates to market and that everyone involved with the trade should work together. They believe in an open and free trade with some regulation and control, but more importantly, they believe in a free flow of information that can greatly expand our knowledge of ancient cultures.

Hershel Shanks, a graduate of Harvard Law School and founder, editor, and publisher of *Biblical Archaeology Review (BAR),* has been an extreme proponent of the free flow of information with his efforts to get the Dead Sea scrolls published and information about them available for other scholars. (See "The Dead Sea Scroll Monopoly Must Be Broken," *Biblical Archaeology Review,* July/August 1990.) His position is that it is basically wrong for an archaeologist or a scholar to have an academic monopoly over archaeological information, and has gone on record for all archaeologists and scholars to publish their information in a timely manner. His opinions regarding the Dead Sea scrolls have some validity, as they were first discovered in 1947 and many fragments remain unpublished. He feels this is a case where archaeology is vulnerable to scholars who gain and retain full control of materials and refuse to publish them. Shanks has stated that the team of editors assigned more than thirty years ago to publish the Dead Sea scrolls have done significant work, but their principal accomplishment the last fifteen years has been to successfully prevent other scholars from studying the huge store of as-yet-unpublished scroll materials. He thinks it is time to let other scholars review the material and perhaps form some new opinions and theories regarding some of the Dead Sea scrolls.

Shanks clarified his position in a symposium at the Smithsonian Institution on October 27, 1990, which was titled, "The Dead Sea Scrolls After Forty Years." As a keynote speaker and chairman of the symposium he made the following point:

"I want to make it clear that I have not criticized the scholars for taking time, they should take as much time as they need. My criticism is directed at their refusal to let others see the scrolls. I have not called for the scholars to hurry up their work; I have called for the release of photographs so that other people can see the scrolls. As a matter of fact, a philanthropic foundation has offered $100,000.00 to publish the photographs, and the scroll editors have refused to do this. So my criticism of the scholars is not that they are slow, but that they are monopolists. And with that introduction, I will leave my three colleagues to respond." (See *The Dead Sea Scrolls After Forty Years*, Biblical Archaeology Society, Washington, D.C., 1991, page 75.)

In all fairness to the Dead Sea scroll scholars, perhaps some photographs of some select scrolls will be released prior to this work being published. In an analogous scenario, I think that there are many archaeologists that go from dig to dig and publish nothing, and sometimes years go by before they can do so. I personally think that more international controls should be in place as to which archaeologist should be awarded a dig permit. Perhaps the dig permit, for a proposed future excavation, should be granted with the proviso that they have published their last dig to some degree. Shanks has noted that the hoarding of dig information is tantamount to looting an object from the ground, because the information is lost due to lack of publishing the most basic type of field report.

The free flow of information is a common thread that many Centralists hold, but there are some Centralists that are more restrictive towards the trade. A Centralist I mentioned before is Thomas Hoving, who perhaps favors an open and balanced antiquities market, but one that is heavily controlled. He does suggest an Ethnocentric Nationalist viewpoint, although he stresses that it is legal to buy and own antiquities, he feels that collectors should think more about what they are buying. He has elaborated on the trade from this standpoint and has published the following in the January 1990 issue of *Connoisseur*, page 119:

"Yet, I repeat, it is legal—eminently legal—to buy antiquities in America. You can sleep easy. No sweat. The burden of proof falls directly on the country claiming its patrimony. But, should you buy antiquities?"

Some Centralists espouse this line of thought, but in my opinion this line of thought is flawed, because the definition of the human condition and the moral questions surrounding the trade do not address the problems and the plusses that are inherent with the trade. In contrast to Thomas Hoving who thinks moral issues should control the trade, I think there are many social, economic, and political issues that have had the most impact on the trade and these issues will play the biggest role in shaping its future. Rather than simply saying it is not morally or politically correct to collect antiquities, I think that it is more expedient to look at the current international laws and gauge their cause and effect. I personally think that John Henry Merryman has hit the nail head, regarding the future and regulation of the trade, about the best that anyone has with his economic theories. His principal view of the trades international legal structure, being interwoven with supply and demand, is what needs to be addressed the most in order to reform the trade.

In support of Merryman, I also think that collecting is a part of basic human instinct. In the course of human history, no one has been able to change man's urges to collect and there will always be a market and a demand for antiquities. There really is no battle for the hearts and minds of collectors, as some Centralists such as Thomas Hoving have suggested. The true collectors have always known that the feel and grasp of an object's inner spirit, its beauty, and its ties to our past is the true nexus of the market and this is something that perhaps Thomas Hoving and others have not entirely captured. The true collectors will always collect and they all sleep well at night.

Author's Note: Hershel Shanks's efforts to get the bulk of the Dead Sea scrolls open to a broad-based scholarly community probably helped push this process forward, because in November 2001, Dr. Emanual Tov announced that the bulk of the 900 scrolls and commentaries will be published in 38 volumes. The scrolls were found in caves around Qumran between 1947 and 1956, and after 1991 the publishing project was taken over by the Israel Antiquities Authority. Dr. Tov, the projects editor in chief since 1990, and his team of about 100 international scholars were able to publish about 28 of the total 38 volumes. The books, published by Oxford University Press are titled *Discoveries in the Judean Desert* and offer a richer understanding of the Jewish world during the life of Jesus and insights into what the Hebrew Bible looked like more than 2,000 years ago.

CHAPTER SIX

NFA, Shrimp, and Uncle Sam

Nelson and Bunker Hunt lost their bid to control the world's supply of silver. In a matter of months, the spot price of silver escalated from under five dollars per ounce to about fifty dollars per ounce. At that point, the market began to turn and then collapsed within a few days. The millions of dollars of silver options that the Hunt brothers were holding were suddenly worthless and they began to borrow money to cover their leveraged positions. In the end, they had to liquidate most of their assets and declare bankruptcy. One asset that the Hunts accumulated was their fabulous collection of Greek and Roman antiquities, along with their collection of ancient Greek, Roman, and Byzantine coins. Their collection included pieces that were considered to have an extremely high degree of art and they paid top dollar for some select pieces and coins. As a whole, their estimated twenty-million-dollar collection was perhaps one of the best private collections formed in the United States and it was a pity that the collection had to be liquidated and broken apart.

In 1990-1991, Sotheby's held a series of sales in a glossy five-part catalog that drew every dealer and collector in the trade. The sale was a huge success and most of the lots went for strong prices. The European numismatic dealers like Bank Leu, Numismatic Ars Classica, and Munzen und Medallion bid heavily on many coins. This series of sales marked a point in the antiquities market where superb quality, in combination with artistic style, resulted in a premium price for a particular coin and/or object. Prior to this sale, surface wear played a role whether an item would sell or not, but the Hunt sale defined an added monetary value to the market that was based not only on surface wear or *grade*, but also perceived superior artistic style. The quality of the objects was important first and foremost in determining value, but the market seemed to look for that hidden element called *good artistic style*. The pieces in the five-part auction all drew multiple bidders and Sotheby's was in hog heaven. The auction floor resembled a feeding frenzy and Sotheby's realized strong returns for the Greek, Roman, and Byzantine coin auctions.

The dollars involved resulted in articles seen in the *Wall Street Journal* and the *New York Times*. The antiquities trade now had a high gloss attached to it by Wall Street, and additional collectors started to get into the market. This new gloss to the market really began on March 1, 1986, when Numismatic Fine Arts (NFA) launched the Athena Fund I. This fund was a limited partnership that had a capitalization of $11 million and each investor could buy a minimum of ten units for $50,000.00. NFA was the general partner of the fund and took a management fee on behalf of the limited partners. Merrill Lynch, who underwrote the fund with the Securities and Exchange Commission (SEC), offered the fund to the general public. The Athena Fund was partly the brainchild of Bruce McNall, who convinced Merrill Lynch that NFA would be a reputable company that could fill a dual role as both a market maker and manager. Athena Fund I proved to be a success, but the Athena Fund II turned out to be a complete failure, in part, for the circumstances already touched upon earlier. However, it could be argued that NFA and the Athena Fund I made McNall money and that it was the balance of his financial empire that had all the problems, which in turn, brought the whole thing down with a collapse of real estate loans that had "ghost collateral."

At the time, in the late eighties, no one really made the connection that the probable root of McNall's success was his control of NFA, and that it was this evolving company that was his primary launching pad and capital asset for building his empire. The amazing thing about Bruce McNall was that he was able to turn an old pot of ancient Greek coins into collateral for the acquisition of some, if not most, of his capital assets and why not? The antiquities trade was now big money with big profits, and all McNall had to show his bankers was a corporate balance sheet showing the profits from NFA's coin auctions.

Sotheby's, McNall, Merrill Lynch, and others had now transformed the antiquities trade into a big business and from this point on; there would be no turning back for the trade. In 1990-1991, the Hunt auctions put a new rubber stamp on the trade and a new transformation of the trade had taken place with big business entering the picture. The Hunt auctions brought ancient coins and antiquities into the limelight in a similar context as the French Impressionist markets huge splash in May 1990, with Van Gogh's *Portrait of Dr. Gachet* selling for $82.5 million, and two days later, Renoir's *Au Moulin de la Galette* fetching $78.1 million. Art and money had now become synonymous. Big business would now forever be married with the trade, in one way or another, and specialized collections had now become a focus within the market.

I realized that it was now the time to change direction in the trade and meet the diverse needs of several collectors. I sensed that these collectors were now interested in building collections that would encompass a diverse range of ancient cultures. I plunged ahead and began to concentrate more on objects, rather than ancient coins, partly because the profit margins were always greater for the objects with a high degree of art, but the main reason I focused on the objects is that I found that I began to enjoy handling the objects more and more. The downside for the objects was that they were not as liquid as the coins, as some pieces have to be held for quite some time before they would sell to the right person. Worldwide, there are dozens of auctions for ancient coins and fewer venues for objects. I began to think that perhaps an art gallery would be useful in showing and warehousing pieces for the right collector. The idea of an exclusive art gallery had its appeal and I decided to open a business.

I bought part of a commercial building in Denver that seemed to be developing in an upward fashion. The area I settled on was Cherry Creek North, which was a few miles southeast of downtown and a few blocks north of the recently completed Cherry Creek Shopping Center. This pocket of town reminded me of Munich, with the wide sidewalks and tree-lined streets. The trendy Cherry Creek Shopping Center was very upscale and more businesses were opening up in the area. There was also a gallery association in Cherry Creek North that had twenty-three galleries as members and with the addition of my gallery made it twenty-four.

Later on, I settled on the name Apolonia Ancient Arts, because there is an ancient city named Apolonia in almost all of the "art-rich" countries and Apolonia derived its name from Apollo, who is the Etruscan, Greek, and Roman patron of the arts. Apollo, along with his sister, Artemis, are both hunters and I recognized that deep inside that I was a hunter, and I felt this was a good name so I started to print some business cards.

The property I settled on was in a modern building that was in the heart of Cherry Creek North. There was a nude, full-size bronze woman that could be seen off the corner intersection, which was seen in a running stance with one arm pointing up at my space within the building. The area was full of outdoor art sculpture like this and it was a pleasant addition to the neighborhood.

I eventually acquired enough material to fill the gallery and I installed a number of glass shelves and sealed cases that displayed the objects under a modern halogen light system.

This layout allowed the viewer to study the objects from different angles and it also created more efficient use of the space that I owned. The gallery was set up on an appointment only basis, and the security was excellent, as an elevator could only reach the second floor with a security code. I beefed up the security even more by installing an excellent security system, which allowed me to control the access for the floor I was on, and I was pleased in knowing that it was secure enough to leave it for a month or more on my travels. The gallery proved to be perfect for my needs and allowed me to hit the road whenever I wished.

I later was able to develop an Internet page (www.apoloniagallery.com) that featured several pieces from a wide range of cultures. This turned out to be successful, as people are now able to view pieces at great distances. Over the last few years, the Internet has been a boom for the art world and has allowed small galleries to show pieces at a cheap price. The Internet has also brought the world of collecting antiquities into many homes and has helped expand the market, as many new collectors have entered the market by purchasing their first piece on the Internet.

One day I was doing some research on some Celtic bronzes and I got an unexpected visitor. The visitor was another collector who had been by a few times, and he was finally able to catch up with me. He examined a few pieces and we settled on a package price for three pieces. He gave me his business card and we shook hands and planned to meet again in the near future. It was another typical deal, but the back of his business card had another name that had a name of a business with a Singapore address. It was pure coincidence that I was planning a trip to Singapore in a few months. I wanted to make some new contacts there and so I put the card in my address agenda and forgot about it.

Checking into the Carlton Hotel in Singapore, I unloaded my luggage, took a shower, and got some sleep after the five-hour plus flight from Tokyo. The hotel was impressive with great service, spacious rooms, fantastic food, great views, and it was located near the metro station that I could take almost anywhere in the city. I opened my agenda and pulled out all the names I had for Singapore. I ran across that business card and decided to call the name that was written on the back. The business I contacted was Lotus Sutra Antiques on Holland Avenue, which was a located near the university. Taking my city map, I walked over to the subway for a quick look at what they might have. The subway was amazing and unbelievably clean, not even a gum wrapper could be seen on the street outside the station. There were marble entryways and air conditioning within each car. The cars were so clean in an antiseptic sort of way that, in contrast, I remembered many a dentist and doctors office that couldn't compare. A gang tag with spray paint was punishable by six months in jail and a huge fine. Public humiliation was not unheard of and the offender would be caned in public. Years later after my first visit there, an American teenager made the international news and a scandal for the government of Singapore developed, as he was caned for malicious mischief.

Thirty minutes later, I found myself in a small shopping arcade and the gallery was a small one-room affair. They had a few pieces that seemed to be priced well. I purchased several small Asian antiquities that were authenticated by a professor who was affiliated with the nearby university. The prices were right and they wrapped up the pieces for travel. One piece was a small bronze torso of a Buddha. This piece was about four inches high and it still had the original casting core on the interior. It was from Ayutthaya and dated to the fifteenth-sixteenth century. Ayutthaya was the ancient capital of the Kingdom of Ayutthaya that was founded by King Ramathibodi I, circa 1351. Ayutthaya became powerful and overran the Khmer Kingdom and forced the abandonment of the capital, Angkor. The people of Thailand now visit the site with a great deal of reverence and regard the Kingdom of Ayutthaya as their ancient capital.

On my way out the door, I bumped into a man in his late forties that was walking into the shop. He was dressed in a light shirt and slacks like most of the locals and he looked like an American expatriate. He excused himself and asked if this was my first trip to Singapore. His midwestern accent gave him away and I was thinking that he could be from Chicago.

"Yes, but after a few days here I feel as if I have been here before," I replied as I extended my hand out for a handshake.

He quickly grasped my hand with a firm grip and said with a slight grin, "No pun intended, but you obviously like old objects from the past. Are you a collector or a dealer?"

"Well, I'm a little of both. Sometimes I'll sell an object right off. Sometimes I like to keep an object for a while before I sell it. Sometimes I'll keep an object and not sell it at all. I'll leave it up to you to decide if I'm a dealer or a collector!" I said with a chuckle.

"Spoken like a true lover of ancient art! You obviously know what you like and know what you want to buy and sell. Myself, I am a collector of small Thai bronzes and I like Japanese silkscreens," he said as he placed his hand on his chest.

His subtle gesture accentuated his love for the art world and was a refined way in expressing his passion as a collector. I knew then that perhaps this man had a great deal of knowledge relative to ancient Asian cultures and enjoyed collecting. It would be interesting to pass some time with him and at the very least, gain some new knowledge and insight about a culture that I knew very little about.

"I have not had lunch yet. Do you know a place nearby where I can grab a quick bite to eat?" I asked.

"Yes, I do and it has air conditioning. I am not in a rush today and I took the day off. Come, let's go and have a nice Indian dish only a few minutes away by cab," he said with a face that was friendly and disarming.

"By the way, my name is Bill Stevens and I work for Uncle Sam," he said with some bravado.

I replied, "OK, Bill. Whatever you say. Does this mean you're going to audit me now?" I laughed.

"No way, but the few Americans that live here year round all think like you do in some ways. They sometimes view me in a negative sort of way. Anyway, I'm starved."

We walked out of the building and quickly caught one of the many cabs that ply the area around the university. The restaurant was small but bright and the air conditioning was welcome. The temperature shot up while I was in the antique shop. The air conditioner was one of those giant water-cooled monstrosities that was mounted in one of the side windows. Its placement allowed one several unobstructed views through the windows that ran along the front towards the street. The white linoleum tile was spotless and the plain white walls complete with photos of wild jungle animals and hunting scenes added a touch to the place that reminded me of a scene with Martin Sheen in *Apocalypse Now*.

This scene was at the beginning of the flick were everyone was sitting around a small dining table in this spotless trailer, surrounded by stuffed animal heads and a trophy case complete with cigar boxes and hunting trophies, eating jumbo prawns, and discussing the termination of Colonel Kurtz with extreme prejudice. I hoped that this guy Bill wasn't heavy enough to discuss terminating anything or anyone like Colonel Kurtz. He seemed more like a bean counter type, but I was soon to learn he was much more than that and bean counter types can be grossly underestimated.

"So Bill, have you been here long in Singapore?" I asked, as I stabbed my fork into the huge and spicy buttery shrimp that was unbelievably succulent. I thought I would open the conversation and see what Bill was all about. I felt his interest in Asian art was genuine so I decided to have lunch with him and, as usual, I was in my hunting mode so I decided to begin here in Singapore with him. He was also an American, which was important, because those of us that travel frequently outside the US often trade information. We also like to size up the locals, which really is our national pastime while traveling abroad. I guess that all makes us feel a little bit more secure while we are in countries that are a world away from home.

"I have been here for about three years and have acquired a taste for Southeast Asian art and I look for pieces on my time away from the office," he said.

"Do you have an extensive collection?" I asked as I popped another shrimp into my mouth.

"Yes, I have several nice stone pieces, bronzes, and a few ceramics. The Khmer and Post Gupta cultures I like the best. I like the various artistic styles between cultures, such as the Bayon and Angkor Wat artistic styles that are seen with Khmer art. I also am attracted to the minute detail and erotic carving that can be seen on many Indian Post-Gupta pieces, especially the red sandstone pieces," he said while cutting his large shrimp in half and downing the other half in one bite.

"Have you done any buying or selling at auction? Have you consigned anything to Sotheby's or Christie's?" I asked in between bites.

"No, but I have a few of their catalogs to use as reference for pricing and to see different styles of carving. I think you can learn a lot by just having the catalogs and viewing all the different pieces."

"I couldn't agree with you more. One can learn a great deal by just collecting the auction catalogs. What is it that you do here, Bill?" I casually asked.

"Well, Kevin, I am a spook," he said with a chuckle.

I then promptly choked on my next shrimp. It felt that it had lodged in the back of my throat and I had to dislodge it with a couple of coughs. The butter began to dribble down the side of my chin and I had to recover with a table napkin over my mouth.

"You mean CIA stuff and all that cloak and dagger business?" I asked slightly short of breath.

Bill laughed slightly and promptly answered, "Well, yes, but its mostly all information gathering. Financial and economic data mostly. Singapore is a hub for trade and we track ships and their cargo. We like to see what goes where and how. If a freighter is running low in the water and its destination is Karachi or Damascus, an arms shipment with heavy weaponry is not out of the realm of possibility. It's actually interesting to see our electronic capabilities in action and they can lead us here, and there, and everywhere. I am getting bored with it though, and I'm finding my art diversions are becoming more of a challenge," he said with that now familiar grin.

"Well, Bill, it sounds like interesting work and I can see how some of the locals here would view you in a suspicious manner, but please don't tell me more of this stuff, OK. I'm an art guy, not a government guy," I said as I put both of my hands up towards Bill and showed him my palms.

"Sorry, Kevin, but I always like to put the question out to all the American businessmen I meet here in Singapore and that is—*I can open a few doors for you in the art trade and I only ask that you be an extra eye. In other words, if you ever run across or hear of any undesirables that would be a true danger to our country, just let me know, OK? I know the trade you are in probably takes you to many countries and you have contacts that may not be mainstream, watch and listen, and something may come your way.*"

With that revelation I sat in my chair totally stunned not knowing what to say. Bill then calmly pulled out a card from his shirt pocket and said, "Call me whenever you want. No strings attached and if you ever need anything, I'll be there."

The card was impressive with a large gold and blue shield in the middle with an eagle's head at the center. His name and the name of the "company" were in small fine print at the bottom. There was no title or position on the card like "Vice President" or "Director," only his name and four telephone numbers. I really had no way of knowing how high up Bill was in the agency and exactly what his true function was within the company. The card didn't reveal this from simply looking at his card.

"Bill, look, I'm truly impressed with what you do and I'll take your card. If something comes my way, I'll call you. If you don't hear from me in this regard then I'll have nothing for you. You may hear from me relative to the art trade more than anything else, fair enough?"

With that, I extended my hand and he grasped it firmly and I paused, still holding his hand, and looked him straight in the eye. This was a technique I perfected in Pakistan when I wanted a straight answer, and I said, "Bill, I don't know exactly what you do for the company and how you fit in the mix, and if in fact Bill is your real name, but I'll try to help only if you help me to some degree and not bring me any trouble, agreed?"

I then shook his hand and let it go. At that moment, I knew that we could trust one another. Bill with that sly smile, also paused for a moment, and looked at me. His dark hair seemed to glisten with that hair gel in the light of the restaurant, and he calmly said, "No problem, and you are right. Bill isn't my real name, but don't worry, and all I'm saying is that you have another friend if you need one, and you can depend on me if you get in a jam or ever have a problem, especially if you are in a place where there are no flushing toilets! Ha! Ha!" Bill chuckled.

I had to laugh to and raised my glass to his in a toast and I exclaimed, "Here's to running toilets!"

CHAPTER SEVEN

It Took My Breath Away

The mob cried for blood. The young Thai kickboxers gave it their all in the final third round, their bodies lathered with sweat as they traded punches with their small eight-ounce gloves and kicks with their bare feet. The music, slowly building to a crescendo from the small ringside band, also brought the crowd up to a lathered frenzy. The Thai military had ringside seats on one side and I was on the other side of the ring in the tourist section here in the run-down arena that was Rajdamnern Stadium. The age of the building seemed to make the event more of a spectacle and created an aura of electricity. The few tourists here were not exactly off the Carnival Cruise Line ship in Miami. They were mostly single men enjoying a break from their sex tour. They all had money on the line along with the locals, either for the red or the blue corners that represented a particular fighting school. The crowd would bet with one another and a Thai yearly wage was not uncommon. The ringside seats, although separated from the bulk of the crowd by a steel chain link fence, afforded sparse protection from the frenzied crowd that tended to get real unruly from time to time.

Suddenly, one fighter would muster an elbow to the ribcage and the crowd would yell, "Yeeeeee! Yeeeeee!"

The other fighter would respond with a roundhouse kick to the side of the head and the other half of the crowd would scream, "Yeeeeee! Yeeeeee!"

The young twelve-year-old fighters would keep it up until one made a mistake and he went down in a rumple of sweat and blood. In this case, it was the blue corner that came out on the short end of the stick. The boy in the red trunks caught him with a hard punch to the midsection and folded him over in an instant. He went down hard and his head hit the mat with a jarring thud. The crowd went crazy as the referee stopped the match. It was not unlike a scene with Robert de Niro in *The Deerhunter.* Some things never change here in Southeast Asia, because like that flick, the betting never abated and there always was a winner and a loser. Like the movie, I wasn't so sure if the loser would be able to enter the ring again.

The break allowed a young Thai military officer to ease up behind me and he said in perfect English, "The general can see you tomorrow at the Oriental Hotel at the Bamboo Bar. Be there about 3 P.M. Agreed?"

I said, "No problem, I will be there."

He then placed his hands together in a Buddhist prayer fashion with his good-bye. The Thai military were all devout Buddhists and crime here in Thailand was very low because everyone sees Buddha everywhere. The Thai people generally wear a small gold Buddha and chain around the neck. The military was here at the match in force because many of them sponsor trainers for the kickboxing. Young boys are recruited at an early age and spend years training for one fighting season. It's no secret that many of them join the Thai military later on in life.

Bill Stevens had advised me to come to Bangkok and pick up a few choice pieces. I felt our chance encounter was cordial and I decided to take him up on his offer. When we finished our meal at the restaurant, Bill gave me the name of a Thai general who was known to have an extensive collection of Southeast Asian art. Rumor had it that he had contacts in Cambodia that could smuggle pieces into Thailand, and then into the world market. I really felt that this was none of my business, as long as he offered me pieces here in Thailand that could be legally exported. I had no idea if those pieces were here in Thailand one day or one century, as his pieces were not documented in any fashion as to exactly when and where they came from.

In 1991, the Cambodian government was just beginning to photograph their art objects and clear their ancient sites of land mines. Even today, tourists should be extremely careful while visiting there, as many of the trails and groves near the ancient sites still have mines and have not been cleared. It's no accident that most of the tour guides at the temples of Angkor Wat are missing feet and legs.

This was my second trip here so I had a basic knowledge of the city. My first visit here was in 1984 and I came as a tourist to explore the city and the surrounding countryside. I came with a friend named Ernie Medrano, who was into world travel and like me, was interested in visiting all the tourist sites that Thailand had to offer. During our third night in Bangkok, we had dinner with a friend of Ernie's named Linda Shirley. Linda's mother was a member of the Thai royal family and her father, Jack Shirley, was an American. Jack was in his late sixties and owned the Madrid Bar in Patpong. They joined us for dinner and we talked a great deal about Thailand and its future.

Jack had a colorful past, as I learned from Ernie prior to dinner, in that he was with the CIA for twenty-five years in Southeast Asia during the Vietnam War. I really didn't talk about this and I certainly didn't bring up his name with Bill Stevens, but I did learn that he was the man who was principally responsible for bringing Charles Sobhraj to justice after an extensive worldwide manhunt that encompassed a dozen nations. This Sobhraj was one of the world's most feared international criminals next to Ilich Ramirez Sanchez, otherwise known as Carlos the Jackal. Sobhraj was immortalized in Thomas L. Thompson's book, *Serpentine,* and was known to have killed a countless number of people without so much as a qualm. Many law enforcement officials and journalists regarded him as the worst serial killer in Asian history, a dangerous distinction for an even more dangerous individual. Given that Jack was instrumental in placing him under arrest, I had a great deal of respect for him.

In order to help bring Sobhraj in, I often wondered if the CIA independently decided to bring the full weight of its resources to bear in the effort. I learned years later that this might have been the case, this from a contact that was under Frank Anderson. Anderson, who was one of the successors to Jack Shirley, later became CIA chief of the Near East-South Asia desk. Jack and Anderson both had many undocumented successful operations for the agency in Southeast Asia and this was due, in part, to their people skills and personnel in the field, rather than their reliance on high-tech hardware.

Jack told us many things about Thailand that night at dinner, so I had a good grounding about the country prior to my second visit here. He was also kind enough to offer the Madrid Bar, in the heart of the sex district in Bangkok, as a place of refuge. This nondescript quiet bar in the middle of noisy Patpong, with all of its sordid massage parlors and go-go bars, had bedrooms upstairs and twenty-four-hour guards.

"If you ever have any trouble, go to the Madrid Bar and you will be OK," he said with a steady gaze as we wrapped up dinner. "And don't do anything in front of a mirror in any of the massage parlors, or you could be the next actor in the latest Thai dirty movie," he added with a slight smile.

"Don't worry, we're not here to do anything crazy," I said with a chuckle.

I then shook his hand good-by and called it a night. Making our way back to the hotel, I remembered Jack's comments about the Madrid Bar and I realized that this bar was probably a CIA safe house and I kept it in the back of my mind. It was a good gesture by Jack Shirley and I will never forget his kindness and concern for one of his fellow citizens.

This trip though, was different, because I was here not to play tourist. I was focused on finding some objects and I was on the hunt. The general couldn't be a better contact to have and Stevens probably gave me his best contact. I slept well that night at the Sheraton Royal Orchid Hotel, knowing that tomorrow could be a big payday. I would also have to be a little more careful, as there was some recent civil unrest in Bangkok.

The following afternoon, I entered the lobby of one of the finest, if not the finest, hotel in the world, the Oriental Hotel, Bangkok. It was situated along the Chao Phraya River, just down a few kilometers from my hotel, so I decided to take a water taxi from the hotel dock. I entered the Oriental's grounds from the riverside, passing the opulent swimming pool, and found my way through the lobby and into the main lobby bar, the Bamboo Bar. On the way, I was given a cool refresher towel and a complimentary glass of cool mineral water. The humidity was intense this part of the day and everybody in Bangkok that was fortunate enough to have the means and the opportunity was inside under air conditioning. I paused for a moment admiring the opulent lobby, and then I saw that there were three men seated at a table near the bar that were in civilian cloths. I recognized the young officer at the kickboxing match and he waved me over. All three men stood as I approached and I shook all their hands in a warm greeting. The mature, older man of the three motioned to a fourth seat at their table and I moved forward to take it. They all had friendly faces and were basically as friendly as most of the Thai people that I had met in Bangkok. There were no pretensions here; Bangkok had its charms and the people are unquestionably the most friendliest in the world.

The young officer opened the conversation with, "Mr. Stevens hopes you are having a comfortable time here in Bangkok. This is General 'R.' The general wishes to remain anonymous, but you can contact him again through me if you wish."

"Thank you very much for meeting with me. I am here to purchase some fine pieces and I will try to meet your price. Is it OK that I buy the first round of drinks?" I said with a chuckle.

The young officer translated for the general and they all seemed to like my answer. The general laughed and said, "No, no, no." The general, casually dressed in a black polo with tan slacks, waved with his hand and a stunning Thai waitress suddenly materialized from nowhere. The baby oil on her tanned skin seemed to exude a raw sensuality.

He said to her in that singsong Thai dialect, "*Singha, Singha.*" She then turned to get the drinks and they noticed as I watched her walk away.

The general then spoke to the young officer and he said, "The general thinks you have good taste. He thinks that you will also like what he will offer you."

The general liked to cut to the chase. I suddenly realized that there would be no picking or choosing, which is normally the case when objects are offered. The general would perhaps offer me a few pieces, or perhaps even only one piece, as a starter for doing business. There would be no chance to pick over and accept or reject from a myriad of pieces.

I was to learn later that this is the way that the most important dealers in the antiquities trade operated-they only gave you one opportunity to do business, not only because it was a privilege to do business, but it also meant that their pieces were important enough to eliminate the picking and choosing process.

The waitress brought the ice-cold *Singha* beers and I raised my glass to the group with a toast, "Here is to good business and to good karma."

I touched glasses with them all and the young officer once again translated. I was hoping he would like the "good karma" part, as I felt the general might have a thing for fate and the role of Buddha guiding one's journey to perfect bliss in everyday life.

The general then touched my glass again and started to rattle off Thai with the young officer. The young officer turned to me and said, "The general wishes to offer a piece he has had for some time. It is a fine piece and one he is sure you will be pleased with."

"I am pleased you have decided to do some business with me. I know that you do not know me, but I assure you I will protect your name and I will be dependable with payment," I replied.

The young officer translated and exchanged a few more words with the general and he said, "The general is pleased with what you had to say. He says you should pay in U.S. dollars, cash only and we will exchange the piece for the money." With that answer, the young officer placed a photo on the table.

I picked up the photo and it revealed a magnificent tan sandstone head that was finely carved. Upon closer inspection, the image appeared to be a fine Khmer piece that was perhaps A.D. twelfth century. The bust had a finely carved tiara with floral motifs in front of a conical-shaped headdress carved with petals. The face could be one of the Khmer goddess, Uma, who was thought to be Shiva's female consort. This was only a guess, and the face appeared to be female, but at any rate, the head was magnificent and could bring a considerable amount of money on the open market.

"How much do you want?" I blandly replied. I didn't want to convey the impression that I was excited about the piece. I knew I had to regard the piece as an everyday offering if I was able to get the right price.

"The general wants the price on the back of the photo. Is that agreeable to you?" he asked.

I quickly flipped the photo over and the number was a complete surprise. It was a gift. I knew then that perhaps the general wanted to read my face as I looked at the back of the photo. Very clever.

I calmly replied, "No problem, I need till tomorrow this time to get you the money. I like the piece and I think your price is fair. I will not try to bargain and I only ask that you remember this next time."

I extended my hand to the general and he shook it with a firm grip. The general seemed satisfied and then stood up, shook my hand again and excused himself by saying in broken English, "I have pressing business, hope to see you again, please excuse, good-bye."

The general departed with the other man who didn't say a word, and I took this man to be a bodyguard or maybe he was his driver. I was then left with the young officer, who said, "I will meet you at your hotel tomorrow, this time, and I will bring the piece to your hotel room. You may look it over and please bring the money. The general is pleased with you. See you tomorrow and the general has an open bar here. Enjoy another *Singha* if you wish," he said with a friendly look.

We said our good-bye and I thanked him for his perfect English. I sat in the bar and reflected in what I had just accomplished. The head would surely sell for twice or maybe three times what I was paying. More importantly, I had met a new contact, one that I could continue to do business with in the future, and this group appeared to be very polished and professional. I was sure that they were moving pieces that would sell for thousands of dollars and I thought that if I did well with the head, I would be back.

The next day I met the young officer at my hotel and he came with another young officer. He carried a bag that was slung over his shoulder and I could see that it was heavy, because he had a thin frame and his shoulder leaned down and forward from the weight. He carried his load without complaint and I could tell it was heavy, and as a slight bead of perspiration began to build on his forehead, he gingerly sat the bag down on carpet in the lobby.

"Shall we go upstairs to my room and look it over?" I asked.

"OK, OK. It has been a long day for us. We have been busy all day to get this to you. I hope you like it," he casually said.

"I can't wait to see it," I replied.

I then patted him on the shoulder and we made our way up to my room. The two Thai men followed me into my room and I motioned that he could lay the bag down on my huge king-size bed. The man carried the bag to the bed, and with the help from the other Thai man, they placed it on the nearest corner. The bed gave way from the sheer weight of the huge stone piece. My excitement grew and my heart began to race when I saw how the bed moved down from the weight. I thought this piece could be bigger than life size and far more monumental that what the photo could convey. If this were so, the head could be worth perhaps four to five times more than what I agreed to pay.

Both of the Thai military men then struggled to pull the head out of the bag. The tape and bubble wrapping gave them some difficulty, but they soon had the thing free and it was placed on top of the bag and all the wrappings. They then stepped back and what was revealed took my breath away. There, laying face up was one of the most magnificent gray sandstone Khmer heads that I have ever seen. The style was classic Angkor Wat, perhaps A.D. twelfth to thirteenth century, and the carving was minute with very few chips or cracks running through the piece. The face was serene and conveyed a feeling of eternal bliss, but what really got my blood boiling about the bust was that not only was it in mint condition, but the carving had exceptional detail in the tiara that could not be seen in the photo. It was dead center perfect, a masterpiece, and worthy of any museum in the world and a piece that any collector would love to possess.

Upon closer inspection, the patina was rich, with a dark brown color that was matted over the infinitely detailed gray sandstone. The patina was mixed with some tiny minute black dendrites that were seen here and there over the outer surfaces. The patina did not extend over the break at the neckline, but I could see that the patina and the water leeching extended into the sandstone for about a quarter inch, from the outer surface into the area were the stone was recently exposed at the break. With ancient art, patina is everything, and this meant that it would take an extremely long time for water to penetrate into the stone and discolor the stone deep past the outer surface.

Sandstone is rather porous and this patina was a mark of its authenticity. The piece would have to be carefully drilled and a pin and base added, but this was only a minor detail. The piece was magnificent and it looked great no manner how it was displayed.

"I like the piece and I have the money for you," I said as I stepped back from the bust that seemed to be alive from a short distance. I then moved towards my room safe and removed a packet of money that I had prepared the night before. I counted the money out on the desk that was situated next to the windows that looked over the silted Chao Phraya River that ran through the center of Bangkok. The money seemed like only paper compared to the worth of what was lying on my bed and in many ways, that piece was worth infinitely more than money. It connected men to the gods and I could see that when the Thai officers looked at the piece, they seemed to regard it as something other than stone. I could see it in their eyes.

"Good, Mr. Cheek. The general will be happy. Use this bill of sale when you leave Thailand. Good-bye and may Buddha shine down on you," he said with that now familiar placing of the hands together as a sign of Buddha.

Both men promptly left and I was now alone with the bust. Upon reflection, I didn't know the general's name, nor was it important really, but what was important was that the piece was now in my possession. I moved over to the piece and lifted it up. The weight was enormous and was much heavier than I expected. The piece was indeed larger than life size. That thin, wire-like Thai officer was tougher than he seemed, in lugging the bag around all day to get it to me, especially in the heat of the day. I was surprised that he could carry it at all. I thought that this would take a box with some luggage carrier that had wheels. As long as I had the wheels, I could manage it OK.

I then began to examine the head again and for one split second I thought the piece had smiled at me. Three weeks later in New York, I sold the head to a private buyer, complete with its new stainless steel pin and marble base. Fortune had smiled down on me and I was able to get beyond what I expected, but I knew the piece would bring a strong price because I had a feeling that Carlton Rochelle, who was the department head for Southeast Asian Art at Sotheby's in New York, would have enjoyed the piece. I thought the piece would fit his exquisite taste in Southeast Asian Art, as the piece compared to and exceeded many of the objects that he placed in his auction catalogs at Sotheby's. I often wondered how much Sotheby's misses due to deals in the private art market, but eventually they would probably get to see it someday.

The Buddha had indeed smiled down on me, and in the process, I regretted having let the piece go. The piece seemed to be pulling at me for weeks after I had sold it, but I needed the money in order to buy other pieces. In retrospect, I owe much to that bust that took my breath away and it gave me the capital I needed to launch my company. For the moment, I was content and I decided to stay close to home for a while.

The golden death mask of King Tutankhamun in 1984. The photo was taken through the glass of the display case.

Outside the Cairo Museum in 1984.

Examining the carved Mayan glyphs at the Temple of the Warriors in Chichen Itza in Yucatan, Mexico in 1982. Note the noticeable wear in the glyph at shoulder height and no and/or little wear in the glyph a few feet higher.

Mint state Greek silver tetradrachm of Seleukos I. Note the Aramaic lettering on the reverse, seen at the bottom with the standing Nike to the left and the Greek victory war trophy to the right. 2.5:1 enlargement.

Massive bronze armlet of the Iranian type, circa 8th/7th Century B.C. Approximately 4.5 inches wide and .5 inches in diameter. (See book cover.)

694

Mint state Greek silver tetradrachm of Athens, minted circa 465 B.C., and consigned to NFA auction XX, March 9, 1988, lot number 694. 2.5:1 enlargement.

Mint state Greek silver decadrachm of Athens, minted circa 470-465 B.C., and from the Decadrachm Hoard. 2:1 enlargement.

The Buddha-like Bruce McNall in 1988.

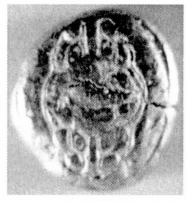

Very fine Greek electrum stater from Miletus, minted circa 540 B.C., and sold to Dennis With. 2:1 enlargement.

Very fine Greek electrum stater from Miletus, minted circa 540 B.C., as seen in Kraay/ Hirmer, *Greek Coins*, no. 588. Identical obverse as the specimen sold to Dennis With and one of four known recorded examples. Note the facing panther heads are seen in a jugate pattern. 2.5:1 enlargement.

The wiry Dennis With in 1991.

Superb Chavin incised stirrup-handle vessel with jaguars. Approximately 10 inches high, circa 1200-700 B.C.

Extremely rare Olmec cylinder vessel, Las Bocas, Middle Preclassic, circa 1150-550 B.C. Approximately 6.75 inches high. Sold in Sotheby's, *Pre-Columbian Art*, Nov. 26, 1985, number 108. This type of vessel was the predecessor for the cylinder vessels that were later produced by the Maya.

146

146
AN ATTIC RED-FIGURE LEKYTHOS
in the manner of the Berlin Painter, possibly by the Tithonos Painter, circa 470
B.C.
the body decorated with the figure of a flying Nike in profile to the left, her wings
outstretched above her body, in her right hand she holds a scrolling tendril, with
meander ground line, tongues around the base of the neck, the rim and outside
of the foot reserved in red. (extensively re-painted)
34.5cm. (13⅝in.)

Provenance:
Sotheby's, London, Antiquities Sale, 12th December 1988, lot 128
£15,000-20,000

Greek Attic lekythos as seen in Sotheby's
London, *Antiquities,* auction Dec. 8, 1994,
number 146.

Roman bronze Horse, circa 2nd century A.D., as seen in Sotheby's New York, *Antiquities,* auction Dec. 17, 1996, number 303. This piece is approximately 2 inches high and has two auction tags attached to the piece. The lot number and sale location is seen and these tags are of the exact type that was attached to the myriad of objects taken in the *Geneva Seizure.*

77

Greek bronze figure of a Running Hero, circa
540-530 B.C., as seen in Sotheby's London,
Antiquities, auction May 23, 1991, number 77.
This is the identical piece subsequently
seized during the *Geneva Seizure* and later
published by Peter Watson in *Sotheby's Inside
Story.*

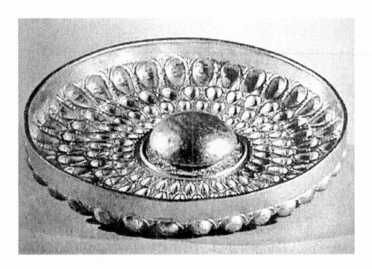

Gold phiale mesomphalos as seen in the Metropolitan Museum in New York. Seen approximately a little less than one-half the actual size.

Corinthian type helmet found at Olympia with the inscription on the left cheek-piece "Miltiades presented this to Zeus." Photo taken in 1985 through the glass of the display case.

CHAPTER EIGHT

And the Spaceman Wore a Helmet!

The coin package I had recently assembled was significant. There were four lifetime Philip II, silver tetradrachms, six electrum hectes from Ionia, an assortment of extremely fine Alexander the Great silver tetradrachms, and one extremely fine electrum stater from Miletus. The Philip II pieces were in virtually mint state condition and the other coins were extremely fine condition or better. In the world of ancient coins, the condition of the coins meant the difference of a few hundred dollars to many thousands of dollars. Generally, extremely fine condition or better was the most desirable coinage for collectors and more often than not, these coins brought a stronger price than pieces that were graded very fine condition. The Philip II tetradrachms themselves were breathtaking and one could even see the minute facial features of Philip II, who was seen waving on horseback on the reverse. These coins were minted during his lifetime, circa 356 B.C., and were probably found in a ceramic pot that protected them from the elements.

The Milesian electrum stater was something to behold and was the lead coin in my package. The *obverse*, otherwise known as the anvil die, had two facing panther heads that were seen in *jugate* form, i.e., the tops of their heads were touching and the bottom of their heads were seen in the opposite direction on the face of the coin. The *reverse,* otherwise known as the punch die, was a rough incuse square design. In antiquity, the minting process involved these two sets of dies and modern numismatists can determine much about ancient coinage, such as whether these dies were interlinked with other dies or not, whether one die was worn and the other fresh, and if the dies developed any flaws from misuse and/or overuse. A *die study* involving this information could determine the size of the issue, the first and last issues that were minted for the series, and most importantly, link and tie dates together within the archaeological timeline. Ancient coinage is one of the single most important links that historians and archaeologists have in helping to date certain events and builds on what we know about a certain event in ancient history. They truly reflect the real reasons, ambitions, and economic conditions of many cultures and individuals throughout ancient history.

The double panther-head Miletus stater was minted circa 575 B.C., shortly after the dawn of coinage, and this piece was probably the fourth known specimen. Another coin, in the same *grade* and/or condition and from the same set of dies, is lavishly illustrated in *Greek Coins* by Colin M. Kraay, Abrams Publishers, New York, Plate 177, No. 588. This issue was very limited, as there is only one known obverse die, and was one of the first issues created by mankind that depicted an actual living animal, rather than a rough symbolic design. These initial coins looked like a raw lump of metal with primitive designs on each side and it is this type of flan that modern numismatists refer to as being "*dumpy.*" The metal was a mix of gold and silver known as *electrum,* which is a natural occurring alluvial deposit, found in numerous mountain streams in ancient Lydia that is now in western Turkey.

This region was also known as the fabled kingdom of King Croesus (circa 560-545 B.C.). Herodotus (Book I, 94) refers to King Croesus as minting an extensive electrum coinage and then being the first to separate the metals into pure gold and silver issues. Many historians also think Lydia was the region in antiquity known as Colchis, from which the myth of the *Golden Fleece,* the object sought by Jason and the Argonauts, was thought to have originated. The idea of a golden fleece is not so remote, as the ancient Lydians are thought to have stretched sheepskins across mineral-rich streambeds, in order to capture fine gold particles from the frigid moving water. In this early stage of minting coins, ancient mining technology was not very refined, as the concept of coinage was just taking hold in archaic Greece, circa 540 B.C. The metal composition of the electrum coinage is also very analogous to the natural-occurring electrum metal and surviving ancient electrum vessels that were produced in the region.

It can be firmly stated, and other numismatists would agree with me that:

"It was this series of early electrum coinage that set the stage for modern trade as we know it, and created the foundation and rise of the modern economic capitalist state that we have today, such is the historical importance of this coinage."

I could have easily placed these coins at auction and realized a tidy profit, but I decided I wanted a quick turnover and in the process, establish a relationship with someone on an ongoing basis. This thought occurred to me, as I was returning back to Denver from one of my many skiing trips in the mountains. A friend of mine, Herb Klug, who had a successful restoration business in Denver, recently said that a guy named Dennis With was now interested in ancient coins. Klug further shared with me that With specialized in United States and World coinage and he wanted to diversify his portfolio.

With had recently leased space near me in the Ptarmigan Place complex at 3773 Cherry Creek Drive North. In 1987, he changed the name of his company to Legacy Investments and some of my collectors said he filled his office with expensive leather furniture, a huge walk-in vault, and a state-of-the-art security system. They noted that his swanky new office was a far cry from his old shop that was in the now extinct Cinderella

City Shopping Center. The contrast was one of white linoleum, starkly lit chrome aluminum display stands, and silver bullion bars mixed with low grade Spanish Colonial gold coins and baseball cards, to new Berber carpet, oak and brass cases with recessed lighting, and high quality U.S. and World coins in plastic cases that each had an individual grade. In the coin world, these hard plastic cases are called *slabs,* and generally contain U.S. and World coinage. Each slab would also contain a certificate, from an accreted grading company, with an identification number that could usually be seen through the clear plastic. Dennis had basically made the transition from selling baseball cards to U.S. and World coins in slabs.

With's wife, Anna, was from Costa Rica and was a beautiful and vibrant woman. She seemed to advertise, with her tasteful attire, the success that Dennis was now enjoying in the coin market. I was impressed with the woman behind the man and that helped to tip the scales in my decision to meet with them and present the Miletus coin package for their expansion. Dennis had, on the face of things, come a long way in a short time and started as a sales clerk for a Denver coin dealer. He then, in the mid-seventies, opened his own shop, Collectors Coin Exchange, in the cavernous Cinderella City Shopping Center.

It was now the spring of 1991 and the Hunt ancient coin auctions had just taken place in New York. I had met both Dennis and Anna briefly a few months earlier at a coin show in Los Angeles and was impressed with the quality material that Dennis was selling at the show. I also learned, at the L.A. show, that Dennis had just formed a limited partnership fund in the same context that Bruce McNall formed and managed the Athena Fund I and II with his company, Numismatic Fine Arts. With would have the money to buy my coin package, provided that he had a number of investors for his fund, Legacy Numismatics International: Ancient Coins.

I wondered whether or not he would understand the ancient coin market, but I thought my meeting with him would have a fair chance of success, so I prepared a package that showed comparable retail sales values for the coins. These values were based on other comparable coins in the market that sold within the last ten years. I then worked up a wholesale price that was discounted for the entire group. With could then turn a profit for his investment at auction, or sell them into the fund, or resale them to other dealers. If he was successful and clever as to how he placed the coins, I could then have a customer for many more additional packages in the future. It seemed like a good idea to sell him the package so I decided to call him.

I set up a meeting at his office the following day and his office exhibited a flair for the dramatic. Dennis appeared to have put even more money into his office and, in addition, it was set up like a stockbroker's office with cushy leather chairs and cable TV. There were coin counters, huge metal bars both in gold and silver displayed in custom cabinets, and an all important executive style bar behind his heavy oak desk.

Dennis was a thin, wiry individual and tended to be a snappy dresser with a vest and tie. He had a close-cropped blond beard and a hyper personality that was flamboyant and slightly off the wall. Anna sat in on our meeting and looked on with all smiles; Dennis offered me a scotch and water.

I replied, "Sorry, Dennis, how about a Coke?"

He got up from his leather chair and sauntered over to the bar and turning with a wry grin said, "Liquid or powder? Ha! Ha!"

His answer was a total surprise and it took me a second to come back and say, "Dennis I know this is Colorado and we've all had our time in Aspen and Vail, but liquid is fine with me." Dennis then handed me my drink and I began to describe the coin package to him and he in turn described his plans for his coin auction company and investment fund for coinage of all types.

At times during our conversation, Dennis would say things like, "That guy Babcock is smoother than baby shit," and regarding my Denver address, "If you would have pulled up here in a pickup and lived in some dump in Aurora, I wouldn't have let you in the door," and in reference to Herb Klug, "Klug! Klog! Clink!"

At the end of the meeting, Dennis cut me a check. Granted it wasn't a certified bank check, but it was a business check from a well-known bank in the area and it cleared my account two days later. We shook hands and I left his office knowing we both had made a fair deal. I also hoped that the extremely rare Miletus stater would find an appreciative home and that the new owner would at least make an effort to understand the piece, rather than shove it into a safety deposit box as an investment. The image of that coin haunted my memory as I left his office, the double panther heads were a powerful image that were created at the very dawn of coinage. Their power represented a city and a market that was only beginning to engage in international trade and finance, and being a large denomination such as a stater, it was probably created to pay for expensive port fees and shipping. The coin would also serve as a symbol for the city and it would let whoever saw the piece know that:

"Our city is one of wealth and power."

It was minted during a time that truly encompassed the birth of capitalism and the beginning of our free market system. Those must have been dynamic times for them; they must have seen a growth in their economy that was unparalleled, and in comparison, perhaps this growth was synonymous with the birth of the information age that we are now witnessing.

Frank Sternberg in Zurich, who was one of the most knowledgeable ancient coin dealers between both world wars, once told me that:

"Each ancient coin has a story, some stories more exciting than others, but always remember—look first at the coin and who made it, when, and why, and only then, you may begin to understand the coinage."

I was happy to have made a deal, but this one was different and my heart was heavy, because I suddenly realized that a collector might never see this piece. The impact of Bruce

McNall and the new presence of investors in the marketplace had finally hit home and I could hear that all too familiar sucking sound.

The sucking sound came to a crescendo when a few months later in mid-June of 1991, Dennis called me to sell me the coin package back to me. I replied, "Sure, Dennis, no problem, but I will only purchase the entire deal back with nothing missing. If you sold the premium coins and made a profit, power to you, but those coins were sold as a package, rather than individually, and I will buy them back as a package."

Dennis did not speak for a moment and he said, "Well, I have sold the Philip II pieces and a number of the electrum coins and I want to sell you what is left."

I then replied, "Have you or have you not already made money on this deal? I am sorry, Dennis, deliver all the coins and I will buy them all back." I got no response from Dennis and then the phone suddenly went dead, with him hanging up on me.

How weird, I thought, that he would pull this, but I was soon to find out that this was not so weird after all, once I found out the reasons for his wanting to sell the balance of our deal and then, inexplicably, hanging up on me like that. Prior to our deal, I had heard several things about Dennis With, both good and bad, from several other coin dealers that were scattered around the country. I thought that this was probably true for most people that were somewhat successful, so I didn't give this talk much credence, but what I didn't know was that With was scrambling for money to pay Peter for Paul. I was lucky that my check had cleared, because With was now behind his rent for his 2,349-square-foot first floor office and his June rent went unpaid. The weekly trade paper *Coin World,* owned by Krause Publications, was owed more than $13,000.00 for advertising that was for With's coin fund, and one of With's investors in this same coin fund was owed his first payment on a loan of $108,000.00. This investor was a retired doctor, a George Babcock, who loaned Dennis more than $108,000.00

in rare coins, bullion, and gold bars. Dennis got even more creative on July 1, and filed suit against the Quaker Oats Company for dental costs, emotional stress, pain, lack of sleep, and impairment to his quality of life, after he bit down and broke some teeth on some cereal.

In July, With was now feeling the heat from his leasing company and they wanted him to move out, and they filed suit for $8,000.00 in unpaid rent. This would explain when and why Dennis called me in June, because he was now desperate for money, but how desperate would shortly be revealed in what can be described as one of the most bizarre cases in Denver history.

During his transition of moving from his swanky office, With transferred many coins from a local bank vault and brought them to his office. They didn't remain there for long, because on Sunday morning on July 28 at approximately 7:30 A.M., someone made off with hundreds of coins and other valuables. With was later able to describe in the police report that someone as being, *"dressed in a spaceman suit, complete with rubber gloves, gray one-piece suit, and a helmet."*

The police found With in a distraught condition, along with one of his employees, a young woman named Darby Griswold. With was so unwound by the robbery, by one account, that he had wet his pants and was crying uncontrollably. Griswold told the police she never did see With and the "spaceman" together at one time, matching With's statement that the "spaceman" first bound With in another room and then tied her up in the vault with duct tape. With was subsequently able to free himself, trigger the alarm, and then free her from the vault about three hours later. The police got the call about 10:41 A.M., and both With and Griswold then gave completely different descriptions about the size and build of the "spaceman."

The condition of the office was a wreck and the police found coins scattered everywhere; it was not a clean grab and run robbery, and it was hard for the insurance investigators to determine exactly what had been stolen and all they really had to go on was a list that Dennis and Anna had compiled after the robbery. The total on the list came to $1.2 million in gold and silver coins. The insurance investigators grilled the Withs for four days, as Dennis had increased his policy coverage from $450,000.00 to $700,000.00 only four days before the robbery. The FBI's criminal report was later to reveal this, along with Griswold's account that, "all the spaceman could do during the robbery was grunt and point."

She went further to state that these grunts sounded identical to With's grunts. The report also revealed that With had contacted a smelting company, about one week after the robbery, and reportedly asked several questions about melting down coins and forming bars. At this point in time, the FBI was pretty sure that they had their man and they arrested him on October 17.

Shockingly, the U.S. Attorney's office was having trouble with their case against With and moved to have the charges dropped pending further investigation. Their main problem was finding an expert to verify the coins and their values, coupled with the fact that their case also rested on the coins that With sent out to another dealer for sale on October 3. That other dealer was Daniel Kihlstadius from Minneapolis, Minnesota, who telephoned the FBI after realizing that With was sending him about $40,000.00 worth of coins after he had been robbed. The FBI seized the coins and then centered their case around them, not knowing that the coins in question were basically common coins with no distinct rarities. They could not positively match these coins up with the coins that were listed as stolen from With's office, although there were many pieces that matched the exact type, grade, and denomination.

Perhaps more damaging to their case was that they had problems getting a coin expert to positively state without any doubt that these were the exact coins from the robbery, as many of the valuable coins from the robbery were in slabs with their identification numbers, and the coins that With sent to Kihlstadius were in plastic sleeves called *coin flips. Coin slabs* are basically airtight plastic packages that have their own identification number and grade. They differ from a coin flip in that the coins, along with the documentation for that specific coin, are not removable from the slab without breaking them open from the hard plastic shell that encases the coin with its documentation, and in contrast, a coin flip is just a soft plastic square cover that does not seal and may have a small paper insert with the description and grade of the coin.

With was perhaps smart enough to avoid prosecution by sending out some generic coins that were not packaged in slabs, so that he could possibly raise some quick cash, but one of With's four attorneys, William Cohan, says otherwise, and that Dennis was unfairly being prosecuted by Assistant U.S. Attorney James Moran.

Shortly after the case was dropped, Anna and Dennis With disappeared from Denver and as far as I know, are still off the radar screen. For a full year, people would call me from places as far away as Alaska and ask all sorts of questions like; "Do you know where I can find Dennis? What happened with the FBI? Do you know where his wife is from, etc.?"

The third question was a good one, and rumors ran through town that they went to Costa Rica and retired there as hotel operators. I also began to think that perhaps Costa Rica had stringent extradition treaties and perhaps Dennis would know this. I never did find out if George Babcock got his money back and if the other investors in With's coin fund recovered anything. However, I did learn from an article in the *Denver Post* dated June 10, 1993, the following:

A federal grand jury indicted a former Denver coin dealer yesterday on charges of mail fraud and interstate transportation of stolen property. US Magistrate Judge Bruce Pringle issued an arrest warrant for Dennis Charles With yesterday. Court records listed With's address as San Jose, Costa Rica. The indictment included an allegation that With robbed or assisted in an armed robbery of Legacy Investments at 3773 Cheery Creek Drive in Denver in July 1991. In that robbery, an employee testified that she had been told to work on the Sunday the robbery occurred, and that a man in a spaceman suit then robbed the store.

Fortunately for me, I never had any problems with Dennis and it was too bad that things worked out poorly not only for him, but also for some of the people that dealt with him. Dennis perhaps created his own monster and the parallels to Bruce McNall are eerily familiar.

Overall, the ancient coin trade has been very rewarding for me and the majority of the dealers in the trade are honest and hardworking people and like any other business, there are those that put a tarnish on things and they would sometimes give the business a bad name, and then there are those that are a credit to their profession. In reality, the ancient coin trade is self-regulated, as most creditable dealers are members of professional organizations like the PNG (Professional Numismatists Guild) and the ANA (American Numismatic Society). They police the business for forgeries, stolen collections, share information within the trade, and protect the public's best interests at coin shows and auctions. The majority of dealers knew the news of the robbery at Legacy Investments the day after it happened, and Kihlstadius should be commended for calling and alerting the FBI. His actions speak for the majority of dealers that are in the trade, and collectors worldwide should take some note in this.

New collectors to the market will find that many dealers are extremely knowledgeable about the coinage they sell and have extensive libraries that list past auction sales, comparable coins, and collections. Collecting ancient coins is an extremely rewarding and sophisticated hobby and there is no limit as to what one can learn relative to the coins themselves, their history, and the cultures that minted them. Perhaps one day, you may find that stater from Miletus.

CHAPTER NINE

The Jaguars in the Jungle

Buenos Aires in Spanish means "good air," and on this spring day in 1993, its name was living up to its interpretation. The slight cool breeze held the scent of a strong lavender aroma, which came bursting forth from the purple flowered jacaranda trees that were sprinkled throughout Plaza San Martin Park. I was to later learn that the hard wood from the jacaranda trees was used to produce the finest Spanish colonial furniture that is now rarely found in Buenos Aires. Unfortunately today, when a party is interested in Spanish colonial furniture, there are often a lot of fake and composite pieces that are offered to the gringos. Unlike the hard wood from the trees, my hunting adventure here in Buenos Aires was pretty soft and easy. I had an easy walk out of the Sheraton Hotel and I began to make my way up through the park that ran uphill from the Retiro Train Station. The Plaza San Martin Park was the terminus for the elegant Florida Avenue, which was packed with ritzy shopping boutiques and cafes. One could stroll down Florida, do some quick shopping, and then relax in the Plaza San Martin Park at the end of the day. My stay at the Sheraton Hotel located across from the park and opposite the Retiro train station was comfortable and had a relaxing swimming pool that some of the local chicas liked to crash.

My friend, Jay Kehoe, suggested that there was much to see in Buenos Aires and insisted that at one time, BA was a world capital for art and antiques, and that it might be a good idea to go down there on holiday and check it out. He felt that there would be several works of art that would be worthwhile and he convinced me to have a quick look to see what I could buy. Jay was a former airline employee with Pan American and had traveled worldwide in his thirty-eight years of life, so I decided to take him up on his offer. He liked to pick up a souvenir here and there and he had an interest in European antiques. He seemed to know what he was talking about, because I also knew that he had traveled to eighty-four different countries.

We then flew to Miami and connected on a red eye international flight that put us on the ground about eight hours later. Jay could only stay for a few days, but he introduced me to the city and knew where I could find the best cappuccino and men's clothing shops. Of coarse he also knew the best nightclubs, and one night at the disco, New York, New York, was enough for me and it completely wore me out, which for us was a good thing. Closing time is normally 5:00 in the morning, and the ladies in their scantily clad dresses, complete with the look of high heels and no bra, loved to dance all night. The Argentines and especially the Brazilians, love the clubs and it was always a custom there to have dinner around 10:00 P.M., and then go for coffee or drinks at midnight, and then go to the all-important disco at about 1:00 A.M. In South America, this was a normal routine at least three times a week, and sometimes more, particularly if you were living in Rio de Janeiro or Punta del Este. The South Americans love life and certainly live it to its fullest while out on the town.

Day three in Buenos Aires allowed my head to clear and I decided to get down to business. Jay took a cab to the airport, so it was now time for me to go to work. In my hotel room I found one of those tourist guides that are full of tacky leather wholesale shops and ceramic factory discounts. I quickly leafed through it, but something caught my eye, and that something was an obscure listing that illustrated the names of several art galleries that were within the central part of the city. A few lines down revealed the name, *Bas Art Gallery*, with the caption, "Specialists in Native and Primitive Works of Art." The address was M.T. de Alvear 716, and as it turned out, was located one block off Plaza San Martin Park, at the top of the hill near Florida Avenue.

It was another perfect spring day, so I grabbed my room key and headed out the door. I found the business ten minutes later and it was a small gallery with a mix of fossils, pre-Columbian ceramics, and European oil paintings. The proprietor, Jose Arias, was a few years my senior and was a very friendly and jovial sort of guy. He was very knowledgeable, especially regarding pre-Columbian ceramics, and over the last few years we became good friends and he taught me a great deal about pre-Columbian art. He had a feel for the pieces and had a good eye for finding hidden repair and knowing the numerous artistic styles of the various pre-Columbian cultures.

The pre-Columbian cultures spanned over a wide range geographically, from the Olmec and Aztecs in Mexico, to the Chavin and Incas in Peru. These cultures were also intermixed over a broad range of time, with most of them falling from circa 800 B.C. to A.D. 1450. Jose was able to heighten my level of interest in pre-Columbian art that I now am extremely grateful for, and through this interest, I began to see the raw power and the symbolism that each piece and culture was able to convey. This symbolism is seen through the design of the piece, otherwise known as the *iconography* of the piece, and is imbued in all pre-Columbian art, and perhaps this is the main reason why there are so many collectors that are attracted to this type of art.

During the auctions that I attended, for both pre-Columbian art and classical antiquities, it was interesting to see several of the same people that were attending both types of sales. The classical antiquities, from the Bronze Age, circa 2500 B.C., and the pre-Columbian pieces, from the Classical Period, circa A.D.

350, have many similar characteristics of form and design, which at first glance makes it sometimes difficult to define a specific culture that produced a particular piece. This may be part of the reason why these collectors are seen at both types of sales, but I suspect the principle reason is that they simply like both forms of art and have developed a taste and an eye for both *genre* of art. I also think that there are presently more and more collectors that are expanding their interest into more than one genre of art, rather than concentrating on one culture or type of object. This interest in more than one genre of art appealed to me, and I eventually developed a wide interest in all ancient cultures, along with the myriad of pieces that they produced.

Jose was very well connected in Buenos Aires and knew many of the leading families that owned extensive collections. They would often come to him for advice and were active buyers and sellers. His business was busy in town and he was fortunate not to depend solely on the foreign buyers that would frequently look for objects while abroad. His wife, Celia, was an accomplished artist in her own right and had several successful art exhibitions in South America, Europe, and the United States. Her style is a modern sweeping-like style that easily captures the grassy images of the vast Argentine pampas. Most of her paintings are landscapes and they are very popular with the local collectors, and as husband and wife, they both have developed a sense of style in the art world in Buenos Aires. On the face of things, this sense of style seemed to define her school of art, and one day the art world may recognize the importance of her work and other artists like her that are now producing images of the vast landscapes of South America. When I viewed her works, I got a feeling of the grand and isolated Argentine pampas, and these images may also be a reflection of the poor economic condition that Argentina is in today. Argentina is an island on to itself in South America, and seems to be isolated from the modern economic mainstream of North America and Europe. I wondered if French Impressionism could one day be eclipsed by the fresh, bold new look of Argentine Isolationism. Like pre-Columbian art, certain elements relative to this style of Argentine modern art are really just now starting to be understood and known.

It was also in Buenos Aires I discovered that, like Jose and Celia, I enjoyed the art trade principally because I enjoyed the art itself, and unlike most dealers who are in the trade solely for the money, I have felt that I have discovered the key that has made my career a rewarding one—which is the continued enjoyment of the art itself and recognizing that this has become my new standard for success.

That first day with Jose was a remarkable one and it ended with a visit to his private office that was at the rear of the gallery. He wanted to offer me a special piece that he had for a while and he wanted the right person to appreciate it. I knew Jose was a genuine person and this wasn't just some local sales technique for the visiting gringo. The piece he wanted to offer me was a ceramic of the highest quality and the piece turned out to be a dark gray early Chavin vessel produced circa 1400-1000 B.C., with deep, incised decoration. The condition of the piece was mint quality, with no repair, cracks, or chips. With ancient art, as with ancient coinage, condition and patina is everything, and together define authentic pieces that are more desirable and are thus worth more money on the open market. This piece also had *provenance*, i.e., clear historical ownership, and it was in a private European collection for a number of years and imported into Argentina in the early seventies. This piece obviously had been out of Peru for quite some time and Jose not only wanted to make our first deal a great one with a killer piece, but also one that had the added bonus of clear provenance. Although this piece was from the earliest civilization in Peru, circa 1400-200 B.C., and Chavin pieces generally command strong prices in both Europe and the US, we both understood that since this piece had clear provenance it would command even a higher premium on the open market.

The piece itself was a powerful spiritual piece, because the *iconography,* i.e., the images and symbolism associated with a work of art, portrayed two *line design* incised jaguars that were seen on each side of the vessel. Each jaguar was carefully executed and was perfectly balanced on each side of the bulbous vessel that had a *stirrup-type handle* at the top. This type of handle was attached to the vessel so that the potter could remove, or turn, the vessel in the kiln with a long stick that ran through the handle. This would ensure that the vessel would fire evenly in the kiln and would give the vessel a nice even glossy polychrome glaze. In this case, the glaze was a beautiful light gray color that could be seen on the entire vessel. (For another vessel of this type, see Sotheby's Pre-Columbian Art, auction Nov. 23, 1982, no. 24.)

Sometimes with Pre-Columbian ceramics, pieces were misfired because of uneven heat in the kiln, which often occurred because the potters were not able to move the pieces around in the kiln, but the Chavin were able to virtually eliminate this problem because of the simple design of the stirrup handle. Considering that the Chavin may be the earliest culture in South America, circa 1400-400 B.C., the design of the stirrup handle is a significant and ingenious development in the history of pre-Columbian ceramics. The Chavin had no prior indigenous culture to model their ceramics after and their production techniques were independently developed through trial-and-error with a high degree of craftsmanship. They were able to produce ceramics that had a high degree of detail and skill, and more often than not, Chavin stylized art design illustrates animal forms with human traits, which clearly define an *anthropomorphic* form.

The two jaguars seen on this vessel were designed with two upturned heads that had open mouths. The front legs were curved up towards the head and the back legs curved away from the body along with the tail. The legs were somewhat human-looking, but the overall design gave the illusion that the jaguar-like creatures were moving. The two jaguar-like creatures are probably spirit protector deities, with the jaguar being the most powerful image on pre-Columbian art in that they were always perceived as devouring all enemies. The raw spiritual power of the piece was quickly evident to me and this spoke even more for the piece, because this piece was one of the first pre-Columbian pieces that I was to own. As time went by, I was able to learn more about the iconography of the vessel and grew to appreciate the piece and the culture even more.

In reflection, I could not help but realize that this process of growing with the pieces, in terms of enjoyment and knowledge, is exactly what many governments, archaeologists, and politicians want to deny collectors of ancient art today. Until one actually is able to own, touch, feel, and explore their own pieces will one really know what this process is all about, and if a piece happens to be a power piece, then you will not only own it, but also it's power.

That evening, I made my way back to my hotel and my outlook towards the pre-Columbian market had changed. I was happy that Jose and Celia invited me to their home the following evening for dinner and a little of that fabulous Argentine wine. We discussed many aspects of tribal and pre-Columbian art and the depth of knowledge that Jose had towards the pieces surprised me. I remember one conversation that dealt with the theory of *spirit transformation,* which was the idea that one could transform into an animal/animal spirit and vice versa. This concept is a concurrent theme that runs through many pre-Columbian cultures throughout North, Central, and South America. Jose thought that this first originated with the Olmec in Mexico and perhaps they were the first to clearly illustrate this through their art. This made perfect sense, as the Olmec were one of the earliest pre-Columbian cultures in the Americas, and they were also the first the develop new ceramic types such as the cylinder vessel, which the Maya later produced in abundance.

I then added, "This concept is far older and was probably inherent with many Neolithic cultures, ever since man first crossed over the Bering Sea into North America."

Jose would then counter, "Yes, Kevin, but the change illustrated by the Olmec is not what you think, but rather is one entirely in spirit form, not from the physical world to the spiritual world and back again, but rather one depicted from the spirit world itself. In other words, when you see an Olmec stone mask that shows the jaguar mouth and eyes in combination with a human shaped head, this is a representation of the spirit itself, changing in the spirit world, so that the living may change as well."

I responded, "Oh, great wine!" Then we would all laugh and begin to talk about another subject such as the economy in Argentina, Mexican pre-Columbian shaft graves, and the always much discussed Clinton this, or Clinton that.

The night moved quickly and Jose dropped me off at the hotel and as I was getting out of the car, I turned and said, "Jose, I had a really nice time and I hope to see you again."

"Good to meet you also, Kevin, and see you again in the future." Jose replied with a slight Spanish accent.

I was to see Jose many times over the years and he was a good contact, but most importantly, he was a good friend to have in the trade. His contacts and knowledge of the region was very extensive, and I was to learn a great deal about South America from him. I remember one trip in late 1993, he mentioned that in the Triple Border area with Argentina, Brazil, and Paraguay there is a city in Paraguay on the Parana River, Ciudad del Este, that bases its economy entirely on smuggling, marketing fake goods, and illegal transfer of cash. He mentioned that elements of the Muslim community, which is now mostly about twenty thousand Lebanese Muslims, engaged in business where one could pay cash in Ciudad del Este and in turn, take cash or delivery of an item such as a TV or a car in Damascus. This type of trading is known as the *hawala* or *hundee* system where moneychangers in one country received a sum of cash while payments are subsequently made to a recipient in another country. In this capacity, there would be no official trace of money trading hands and the business was done through family connections and/or tribal clans that would even the accounts, sometimes years later. At this point in time in the early nineties, very few people in the United States were completely aware of the *hawala* system of money transfer and its shadowy existence.

On one of my trips into northern Argentina, I was later able to confirm much of what Jose knew about the region and I was certain that there were many businesses there that were fronts for many terrorist groups, which were raising money for their various causes. I was to learn a few years later that one of these business fronts was selling honey from Yemen, which is considered by many Arabs as the finest quality in the world, and this company was later exposed as a front for the terrorist group al Qaeda and its notorious sponsor, Osama bin Laden. This company earned millions worldwide, because of the Arab daily ritual of taking tea heavily laced with honey. Arab connoisseurs claim that the honey from Yemen has its own subtle and distinctive taste.

Jose and other art world people in Buenos Aires were also convinced that terrorists from the Triple Border region were somehow involved in planting the car bomb that blew up the Israeli embassy in March 1992. In that attack, the entire building was leveled and an estimated twenty-nine people were killed, some of whom were Argentine nationals. An even worse car bomb attack occurred a few years later, on July 18, 1994, on the Argentine-Israeli Mutual Aid Association (AMIA). That explosion killed eighty-five people and in both cases, police officers assigned for security on both buildings inexplicably vanished just before the explosions. Jose's gallery was a few blocks away from this more powerful second attack that completely leveled the building, and he said the explosion vibrated the city for miles in every direction. A friend of his, who owned an apartment on the fifteenth floor of a residential building a few blocks from the AMIA rubble, found the bloody top of a human ear on his balcony, along with a thick layer of dirt and various bits of concrete.

After close examination of this grisly item in its plastic

Ziplock freezer bag, I subsequently sent a cable to Bill Stevens advising him that funds originating from the Triple Border region could have financed the terrorist operation in Buenos Aires, as several of my contacts in northern Argentina individually revealed to me the same scenario as to how terrorist money could have tied into the whole mess. I was also uncertain as to who was responsible for the attacks, but my advice was, "Follow the money trail and see where it will lead."

I was able to learn later that Paraguayan and Argentine intelligence (Secretariat of State Intelligence-SIDE) speculated that there were numerous individuals in the Triple Border region that had direct ties to Hezbollah and its terrorist arm, Islamic Jihad. These terrorist organizations were active in southern Lebanon and the Lebanese connection was all too evident in Ciudad del Este. Moreover, the president of Argentina, Carlos Saul Menem, who held power from 1989 to 1999, is of Syrian-Lebanese descent, and because of this, rumors and speculation ran within the Argentinean art community that Menem could have been involved in some capacity with the attacks. It was also no secret in Buenos Aires that Iranian embassy officials had close ties and probable business relationships with Menem and/or his inner circle.

Shortly after the second bombing, several arrests were later made in the Triple Border area with a joint U.S., Argentine, and Paraguayan operation, but the unregulated *hawala* system continued to operate. From 1990 to 2000, the money involved in drug smuggling, fake CD and clothing sales, bogus aircraft parts, and second-rate generic medical supplies amounted to no less than an estimated one hundred million, which is a staggering amount, and this money could mostly have flowed into the accounts of several Middle Eastern terrorist organizations. (See *O Globo*, Sabado, 27 de Abril, 2002, Pirataria S/A-Paraguai, a alma do comercio clandestino. *O Globo* estimated that the annual dollar amount of illegal merchandise from Ciudad del Este was U.S. $1.2 billion.)

In my opinion, and I am extremely certain that this was and is the case, the overall total dollars for the antiquities trade in South America pales in comparison to the lost sales tax revenue, lost interest income to the international banking system, and the lost regional economic development in those countries that condone the unregulated hawala trading system in Ciudad del Este, as this money is routed outside and sealed off from the local banking system and economies in the region.

The "El Barakat Network" established by Lebanese businessman Assad Ahmad Barakat has recently been established as having ties to Hezbollah and an international warrant has recently been issued for his arrest in October 2001. Barakat is the co-owner of one of the largest shopping malls in Ciudad del Este, Galeria Page, where fake CD and designer clothing is offered in abundance. The Argentine police are now also looking for one of the tenants in the mall, a Samuel Salman Al Reda Reda, for his alleged role in the Buenos Aires embassy bombing in 1992. The Argentine police are now finally closing the net and the secret of the *hawala* trading system is now public knowledge, and although many of the Muslims that now live in Ciudad del Este deny that there are direct links there to the scourge of international terrorist groups, they were contributors to international terrorism, either knowingly or unknowingly, if they utilized the *hawala* trading system. What they have failed to understand is that the money in the *hawala* system is interlinked, and that their transactions help to even the accounts of other transactions that may be terrorist-oriented and/or controlled, and in addition, any fake CD and clothing purchases made by the community enters the cycle, as this money probably enters the system at one point or another.

So the Muslim protests in Ciudad del Este of November 2001 that contend that they have no direct link to international terrorism is unfounded, as long as the unregulated *hawala* trading system is a part of their community, and this, in tandem with the drug smuggling, fake property sales, and unregulated transfer of funds, which at some point enters the unregulated *hawala* system that is prevalent in Muslim communities worldwide, wrap the Muslim community in Ciudad del Este into the world of international terrorism. If the Muslim community in Ciudad del Este and other Muslim communities worldwide want to truly sever their link to international terrorism, then they themselves should ban the use of the *hawala* trading system, or at least discourage members of their community from utilizing the system.

In reflection, I was glad to have alerted Stevens about the *hawala* system and the knowledge that I accumulated about this through my contacts, but more importantly for me, I was able to learn a great deal about pre-Columbian art while I was in Argentina. Over the years, I would meet many people in the trade like Jose and it made the travel and the business even more rewarding. The social aspect of the trade also made the business part of the trade a lot more enjoyable, and I was lucky that this became the norm for me. I was not only able to learn about the present cultures of many of the people I was dealing with, but also detailed knowledge relative to ancient cultures and the spectacular art that they produced. In reality, what it came down to for me was that if I wasn't enjoying the type of business I was in, then what was the point? I have always been a firm believer that if one isn't enjoying and making the best out of one's career, then it's time for a change. I was perhaps lucky to realize early on that the trade was what I really wanted to be involved with, and in reflection, my initial trip to Argentina brought out this realization.

From time to time, I found that the press would trash the image of the trade with stories that organized crime was all behind the trade, and that the trade is a multibillion dollar annual business, and that virtually all the pieces on the open market are all from looters. There might be some truth in this to some degree, but in reality and from personal experience, I think the trade is not as grand as most journalists, archeologists, and politicians would lead the general public to believe.

For me, I felt I was lucky enough to look beyond all the politics and all the other negative comments about the trade, and instead focused on handling, looking at, and enjoying the objects. This was why Argentina was such a delight for me and I know that is the way it is for a lot of the other dealers and collectors that are out there.

CHAPTER TEN

Some Things to Look For

The testing process is one of the things within the antiquities trade that sometimes can't be avoided. Once in a while, I would come across an important piece that needed a laboratory test to validate its age and therefore, its authenticity, but before a test is in order, I first make it a point to determine some of the basics about the piece in question. The first thing I look for, especially when considering a purchase, is the overall makeup of the piece. I always ask myself is it complete, or is this object a part of a larger piece, and what type of material is this piece made from. Along with this determination, I carefully look at the piece from all angles and try to determine if there is any repair and/or fill, especially if the piece is a ceramic or terracotta.

If you can, always try to view a piece in daylight as you can see more of the details of the surface, and always remember the golden rule—never buy the story behind the piece, but rather the piece itself.

It is important to note that the term *repair* to a vessel generally means that there may be several original pieces that were fitted together, such as a handle that was attached to the main body of the piece. In contrast, the term *restoration* to a vessel generally means that a section of the vessel could be completely rebuilt and/or a part was created for the vessel, and in this case, the piece is not 100 percent original. If an object is described as being *intact,* this generally means that the vessel has no repair, and/or restoration, and the piece was never broken into fragments. If one is purchasing a piece, it is first important to distinguish this difference if the vessel is being sold with or without these descriptions.

A simple spray bottle with water will sometimes reveal repair and/or fill on ceramics and terracottas. Simply hold the bottle a few inches from the surface and lightly cover it with a thin layer of water. This will sometimes reveal surface discoloration of the clay and may indicate fill in those areas. Also, and more importantly, pay close attention to the rate of absorption of the water. If the water tends to suck into the clay at a very rapid rate and if there is an obvious earthy-like scent, then nine times out of ten, the terracotta and/or clay is ancient. When dipped in water, ancient terracotta and/or clay, regardless if it has been buried in the soil, will emit this earthy scent not unlike the smell of a freshly plowed field. This truly is the smell of antiquity. If the water just sits on the surface and absorbs very little, or none at all, and in combination with the absence of even a minute earthy smell, then the terracotta and/or clay is probably not ancient and may indicate a great deal of restoration.

If the piece is a *polychrome* ceramic, meaning that the ceramic has a glaze over the terracotta and/or clay, pay close attention to the surface to determine if it has been waxed. If it has been waxed, then the water may not readily absorb into the piece. Waxing is normal, especially for many pre-Columbian polychrome pieces, as it brings out the colors of the polychrome and one can see additional detail of any minute line design.

The next thing to proceed with, once you have determined the composition of the piece, is another look at the material it is made from. If the piece is stone, a water test is still useful, because it may reveal dendrites, root marks, and other deposits that are adhered to the surface of the piece. If the stone is somewhat porous, one may also get an earthy scent after the piece has been sprayed with water.

A *dendrite* is a microscopic organism that lives in soils and they attach themselves to the surface of any material that was underground for a long period of time. If one finds groups of dendrites that are evenly distributed on the surface of a stone piece, this may indicate that the piece has not been cleaned and that there is a good chance that the piece is authentic. When one is looking for dendrites, one should always use a strong magnifying glass and they usually look like small black dots. Depending on the type of soil that the piece was found, a dendrite may be so microscopic that only a microscope can detect them, but usually they are often seen with the naked eye if one looks close enough. One should also be aware that an object could be buried for a number of years so that it may acquire dendrites, even though it is a forgery. There are also many authentic pieces that do not have dendrites, because an object may not have been buried in soil and may have been placed in a protective enclosed tomb. Fortunately, the majority of imitation pieces that show fake dendrites are easily created with black paint, which is usually applied to the surface by quickly flecking the paint off a brush.

Once in a while, one can sometimes find a *spall* on the surface of a ceramic. A spall is a small opening usually seen on the smooth outer surface of a ceramic that is normally about one-eighth of an inch in diameter. A spall is formed through a process called *levigation*, which occurs when the clay for the ceramic is intermixed with mineral deposits before the piece is fired. The mineralization in the clay then reacts with other minerals in the soil, and this causes a chemical reaction causing the mineral within the ceramic to burst forth and work its way out of the ceramic. This process can only take place after the piece has been buried over a great number of years and more often than not, the spall hole also acquires a dark black mineral deposit within the hole.

A *root mark* is a delicate fibrous trace or deposit that can be seen on the surfaces of many antiquities, and are usually very easy to detect on pieces that are stone and ceramic. Sometimes, these marks are microscopic and sometimes hide in drapery folds, behind ears, and other undercut areas of a work of art. They are generally harder than the stone that they attach themselves to and forgers often have difficulty in duplicating this natural process. Root marks tend not to attach to ceramics as they do stone, but they leave a fibrous trail or trace on the surface of the ceramic, which may be caused by the acid that is in the root itself. Generally, the root marks found on the surface of ceramics are large and are easy to see with the naked eye. Keep in mind that not all antiquities have root marks, but they are something to always look for.

I once purchased a Roman glass pitcher, circa A.D. second century, which was approximately seven inches high with a delicate handle with a small opening at the top. This light blue-green vessel was about half full of dirt and I decided to carefully use a metal wire to pick it out of the piece. I was able to break the dirt up into small pieces that could be dumped out the open end. I had to be very careful not to crack and damage the vessel, so I took my time, had a glass of wine, and turned the radio on to the jazz station. As I was working on the piece, I found that the dirt that was at the edge of the glass would break away cleanly, and the dirt at the center of the vessel was hard to break up. Upon closer examination of the dirt, I discovered that there were minute fibrous roots that ran throughout the dirt and often placed themselves in-between the dirt and the glass wall. This was part of the reason why the dirt broke easily away from the glass surface and I was also able to see on the inner glass surface, the root mark trails and traces on the inner surface of the glass. The collector who later purchased this piece loved these minute traces and was happy that the piece had not been overcleaned.

In this case, the root marks were not only a mark of authenticity, but they were visually pleasing to look at through the glass and became an added value for this knowledgeable collector, which is why I tell everyone that owns objects the following:

"Never, never attempt to clean objects and always try to preserve elements of the natural patina on the surface, as this

may help to prove the objects authenticity and may add an additional value to the piece in the eyes of a collector."

A Q-tip dipped with acetone will also reveal if a vessel has been repainted, can remove fake painted dendrites and thick overpaint, and expose restored areas of a vessel. Slightly turn the Q-tip over the surface in one spot, and the acetone will quickly remove any surface paint that is not part of the original polychrome glaze. I was once offered a Mayan cylinder vessel that had detailed design work over the entire surface, but the problem was although the cylinder itself was original, the entire surface had been repainted in an effort to deceive the buyer. The painter must have spent hours working on the deception, but the Q-tip dipped in acetone saw through this in a number of seconds. A minute amount is all you may need to create a bare dot, as the acetone quickly penetrates down into the original surface. You may then work a grid pattern, as I did with this piece, in order to determine the extent of the overpainted area. Sometimes it is the simple tests like this that yield the best results.

The next thing to look for is the overall patina of the surface, and one should note how the patina looks before and after a water test. The *patina* of an object is the overall buildup of dirt, dust, mineralization, weathering, etc., that gradually affects the surface of an object, and as a result, there is an accumulation of deposits on the surface that includes oxidation and mineral buildup. One should never rub the water off the surface, as this may remove elements of the object's patina.

With ancient art, the patina is the single most important factor that may determine the authenticity of an object.

There is now a movement among collectors to collect pieces that have a natural patina and some collectors insist on buying pieces that have no restoration and/or repair. These collectors want objects in their pristine or *"as found"* condition, with no surface problems, and this now goes far in determining not only the authenticity of an object, but the value of an object as well.

Surface problems relative to ancient art have to deal with deterioration of the piece and this applies especially to ancient bronze coinage. Bronze tends to deteriorate faster and easier in the ground than gold or silver, and bronze is particularity susceptible to chemicals that leech through the ground that act directly on the outer surface. Worldwide, many farmers are now using chemicals such as fertilizer and other chemicals for insect control, and these have greatly damaged ancient artifacts that are still in the ground. These chemicals literally eat away the surfaces of many ancient objects.

Over the years, I have been seeing more and more Roman bronze coins, including large *sestertii,* that were found throughout Europe that have deep pitting and erosion to the outer surface. These coins were found in fields where the farmers who worked the land liberally applied chemicals to the crops. In this case, the argument that ancient objects are perhaps better out of the ground, rather than deteriorating at a rapid pace while still in the ground, does not sit well with most archaeologists who prefer to leave objects in the ground until they can be scientifically excavated. A solution to this problem may be with the establishment of "free" excavation zones in areas that have heavy chemical application. Metal detectors would be able to operate freely in these zones so that many buried objects may be found, which would thus insure their survival.

The increased demand for ancient objects with a nice patina and pristine condition goes further to advance my contention that there is now a *naturalism* movement among collectors and they are paying top prices for pieces that are seen in their "as found" condition. Several examples of this would be a Moche bronze mask, with a dark green patina and fragments of textiles still attached within the thick patina; a marble Greek Cycladic idol, with a spotty white calcium buildup that is solidly adhered to the original surface; and a terracotta-seated Colima woman, with thick black spotty manganese deposits which are deeply embedded into the surface. This last example is important, because there are many antiquities that have thick mineralization attached to the surface, the most common mineral being black manganese. This is especially true for those cultures that dwelled in western Mexico, such as the Colima, Nayarit, and Jalisco cultures. Most of their pieces have these deposits to some degree and in some cases the deposits are so prevalent that large parts of the vessel would be completely covered, forming what is known in the trade as a *manganese bloom* patina.

Several years ago I attended a conference at the Denver Museum of Natural History, which is now the Denver Museum of Nature and Science that was chaired by Dr. Bob Pickering. The conference was centered on ceramic forgeries from western Mexico and their characteristics. The focus centered on those pieces produced circa 100 B.C.-A.D. 300, by the Jalisco, Colima, and Nayarit cultures. Pickering's arguments seemed sound, but he seemed to have trouble answering the following question that I asked following his presentation:

"Yes, but I realize that there are now very sophisticated methods for duplicating fake manganese patinas on these pieces, but aren't they mostly on the surface? And if you were able to take a pen knife and dig down into the surface and find that the patina has penetrated deeply into the piece, isn't that a good indication that the piece is authentic? Especially if some of the deposits were on the surface and others deeply embedded?"

Pickering could not answer these questions with a clear, "yes" or "no," and I felt that his findings did not completely address this question, and his conclusions appeared to skirt around this point, and in reflection, he seemed he did not want to be derailed from his presentation which stressed that there are many pieces on the market that are fake, fake, and fake. So I let him move on with his question-and-answer session and I didn't bring up my additional points, that there are now even more sophisticated laboratory tests that are now being done to test the age of terracotta/clays, along with their surface deposits, and that there are now many more private laboratories that are now testing more and more pieces.

In retrospect, perhaps I should have argued these points, because there were a number of collectors in attendance and many of them appeared to have lost faith and interest in collecting the pieces. By interjecting some pro-collecting points in a friendly fashion, more information would have been introduced into the forum for everyone's benefit. I felt his presentation, although very credible, was very one-sided towards pressing the issue of fake pieces, and after all, this was the subject of his presentation, but perhaps his presentation was also geared towards the collectors that were in attendance and would possibly convince many of them to seriously stop collecting, and since his presentation was sponsored by the museum, presented at the museum, and advertised as such in the *Denver Post* and the *Rocky Mountain News,* I wondered if this was also an agenda put forth by the museum.

Laboratory testing of ancient art is nothing new and carbon-14 dating has been around for quite some time, but what is new and perhaps many people may not be aware, is that there are many private laboratories that are now in operation and can perform a complete series of tests for about $250.00-$400.00. This price continues to move down, and as more laboratories come on line, I suspect these testing services will drop their prices even more. This is important to the average collector, because it is now becoming possible for them to test many of their pieces if they choose to do so. It also allows many dealers in the market to test pieces that have a doubtful authenticity. These tests are extremely detailed and come complete with scientific printouts, graphs, and magnified photo enlargements. Depending on the type of piece to be tested, some laboratories specialize in one type of piece over another and are better equipped to do so.

Some of the laboratory tests for ancient works of art include:

Thermoluminescence (TL). This test is applied to test the age of the ceramic. A small core sample is heated, which releases energy in the form of visible light that can be measured. This measurement is defined as a form of environmental radiation, which the ceramic has been exposed to since it was fired, and the older the ceramic, the more radiation can be detected as more energy is released.

Atomic Absorption Spectrometry. This test can determine the geographical origin for all kinds of clays. All kinds of clays contain numerous elements such as aluminum, silicon, iron, and in addition, other trace elements in known combinations worldwide. Like a unique fingerprint, this test can provide some answers to a specific geographical origin for the origin of an object.

X-Ray Fluorescence Analysis (XRF). A test that reveals which chemical elements comprises an object, or its parts. This test is useful to determine if a piece is completely intact and is made up of its original parts. The object is exposed to x-ray light and from this sample, secondary x-rays are emitted that is specific to the samples specific chemical composition.

X-Ray Fluorescence Spectrometry. This test can reveal the exact percentage of metal combinations such as gold, silver, copper, and tin. This is an important test for objects that are produced from metal, and can be compared to the ratios found in similar known authentic objects that are from the same culture.

Stereo Microscopic Analysis. This examination can reveal minute microscopic wear and scratches that are on the surface of a piece. This can also reveal modern and/or ancient tool marks, and the natural wear that all authentic antiquities show to one degree or another. Examination of several specimens can also reveal consistent manufacturing techniques and methods of construction.

The tests noted above are the more common and mainstream tests that most of these laboratories can perform. They may also perform some additional exotic tests if they are requested, and one can proceed with several layers of these tests, that together, would provide ample scientific evidence that the object in question is authentic. It is important that if one wishes to buy an object, make sure that the seller will offer an authenticity certificate along with the piece, and that it is sold "subject to" the results from a laboratory test. Most reputable dealers in the trade offer authenticity certificates along with their pieces, and will offer a refund, especially if a laboratory test finds part and/ or all of the object in question was not represented in line with the bill of sale. In some cases, the object in question may be authentic and it may differ in age from one period to the next, and/or part of the object may not be completely authentic, and/ or the material that the object is composed of may not be as represented. These problems are often addressed in advance of a purchase and are questions that one should ask while considering a purchase.

Some basic questions that one should ask while considering a purchase are as follows:

Is this piece Greek or Roman and what period do you think this piece is from? Is this section of the piece original or has it been restored? Is this piece made from this type of stone or another type of stone that you may or may not be aware of?

Always try to remember to ask as many questions that come to mind about an object that you are considering to purchase, and as with any purchase, the more you know, the more confident you will be about the deal, and the more you may then come to appreciate and enjoy the piece. Another thing to always remember, never depend solely on someone's so-called expert opinion, as many of these experts are later often proven wrong, and always remember an opinion is only that, an opinion. Most importantly, always consider whom you are dealing with and who is making an opinion for an object on your behalf. Is this person a museum official, an archaeologist, a dealer, or a collector? Consider if they are "pro" or "anti" private art market, as this may also influence their opinion, along with the possibility that there may be a money issue involved.

When it comes to a purchase, try to get as many opinions as possible, and then get a laboratory test for the object if you are still not comfortable with what many people have to say about the piece. Most reputable dealers in the trade, such as Selim Dere of Fortuna Fine Arts on Madison Avenue in New York, will offer their clients a purchase "subject to" a laboratory test with a minimum deposit, along with an authenticity certificate and a bill of sale, and this would especially apply to pieces that are somewhat expensive and/or are rare. Collectors that are considering purchasing an expensive object on the Internet should keep this in mind as well, and should always consider whom they are dealing with.

Most dealers can also offer you suggestions as to how a piece should be displayed, how and if an object should be mounted on a stand, and how to best care and preserve a piece, particularly if the piece is wood or bronze. One should also consider where an object is displayed, as environmental conditions may sometimes affect the condition of an object.

All of these factors relative to the display of ancient objects is very important regarding their preservation and appraised value, and this especially applies to ancient textiles. These textiles are often mounted on a felt backing and are encased in a plexiglas cases that protects the textiles from dust, insects, and ultraviolet light.

Steve Berger of Arte Textile once commented to me at an art show in San Francisco:

"The moth is the single greatest enemy relative to the preservation of ancient textiles. They can destroy a very valuable textile in a very short time, and textiles are also very sensitive to the penetrating and destructive ultraviolet rays of the sun. Plexiglas filters most of the ultraviolet light and consequently, preservation goes hand-in-hand as to how a textile is mounted and displayed."

Once you have decided to purchase a piece and you are satisfied with all of the technical aspects of the piece concerning its composition, authenticity, and eye appeal, once again be sure to always remember the golden rule—never, ever, buy the story behind the piece, but rather buy the piece itself.

The antiquities trade is a rich and rewarding collecting endeavor and sharing information about the pieces with other dealers, collectors, and scholars is really what collecting is all about. If you decide to collect, keep this in mind and your own knowledge will grow, along with the knowledge that you may someday make your own contribution to what we know about ancient art.

CHAPTER ELEVEN

The Ancient Mentality

In the war to control Afghanistan, the Taliban began to gain more and more ground in 1994. The Taliban, which means "religious students" in Pashto, which is also the language of Afghanistan's largest ethnic group, began to impose their will on all of the ethnic groups they encountered and in the process, they destroyed everything and everyone who stood in their way.

The Taliban were first fostered and supported by Pakistan in order to create a government in Afghanistan that was perceived as not being a threat on their western border. Pakistani intelligence, the Inter-Services Intelligence agency (ISI), now had its big payday, as the Taliban became a viable and formidable force within the country that, as far as ISI was concerned, could be controlled and manipulated. Christopher Hitchens, in the January 2002 issue of *Vanity Fair*, in the article "On the Frontier of Apocalypse" adeptly summed up his perception of the relationship between Pakistan, the Taliban, and the US:

"In the 1980s, Pakistan got a blank check from the US to combat the Russians, and spent much of the check in building up the Taliban. Now it is getting another check and a brand-new interest free mortgage in order to *pretend* that the Taliban are its enemy. It doesn't get any better than this."

It remains to be seen if the Pakistani government will be a solid ally of the western coalition to fight terrorism, by arresting members of the terrorist organization al-Qaeda, by disarming armed Taliban that are trying to escape Afghanistan into the tribal border regions of Pakistan, and by banning ISI from any further support of the Taliban. One cannot ignore the fact that the Taliban received a great deal of aid and arms from Pakistan, but in order for the current military regime to survive in Pakistan, it may have to slowly turn the screws on the radical Islamic factions that are advocating violence within the country. Only time can tell what political change might occur in Pakistan in the coming years, if democracy can be established, and if the people there can all live together in peace. Unfortunately, it may be that many more people will die there in the not-too-distant future.

During Pakistan's drive to establish control of Afghanistan with their support of the Taliban, Kabul became the central focus of the Taliban for the control of the country, with most of the buildings suffering severe damage. The city began to resemble a moonscape and, in the carnage, a great number of the civilian population were killed or mutilated, and this is, in part, why many commanders of the Northern Alliance hate Pakistan, because in their view, Pakistan's aid to the Taliban contributed to the carnage and the deaths of many civilians.

The Kabul Museum suffered in the exchange of mortar rounds and small arms fire, and in fact, a great deal of the museum was destroyed from 1992 to 1996, during the seesaw control for the city between the Northern Alliance and the Taliban. The objects housed within the crumbling structure also suffered, along with the majority of the civilian population. It could be said that the condition of Kabul's population was in proportion to the condition of the museum itself. The museum housed many masterpieces that ran back from the Neolithic, to the Greco-Roman, to the Buddhist and Islamic periods of history. Very few outsiders were able to see Afghanistan during the control for Kabul, but reports began to filter out that many of the objects in the museum had suffered considerable damage and through the carnage, the UNESCO accords (Convention on the Means of Prohibiting and Preventing the Illicit Import, Export, and Transfer of Ownership of Cultural Property) officially remained in place relative to the many countries that surround Afghanistan. This restricted and hampered many objects from leaving the country, as Afghanistan is landlocked, and any objects leaving Afghanistan would have to enter and then leave those adjacent countries in order to enter the international market. Although Afghanistan was a standing member of UNESCO, Afghanistan has not, as of this writing, signed the 1970 accord (Convention on the Means of Prohibiting and Preventing the Illicit Import, Export, and Transfer of Ownership of Cultural Property), which prohibits the removal of artifacts from a country without approval of that country's government.

This clearly meant that the United Nations (UN) and UNESCO were enforcing a treaty that specifically banned ancient works of art from leaving Afghanistan, because by supporting a containment policy with nations that encompass Afghanistan that were both members of UNESCO and parties for the 1970 accord noted above, objects had to enter the market from one of these countries into the international marketplace.

Fortunately, in spite of the UNESCO accords, many major pieces made it out of the country during the battle for Kabul, and are now safely in many museums worldwide. As the Taliban widened the conflict even more in 1997, the battle for the Bamiyan valley began to heat up and the valley changed hands back and forth, just like Kabul did a few years earlier. Carved from a massive cliff face in the valley are the two spectacular Bamiyan Buddhas that stand approximately 120 feet, and the other, which is about one-half mile away, stands approximately 170 feet, and is believed to be the world's tallest standing Buddha. They are thought to have been carved in the A.D. fifth century and Hiuan Tsang, a Chinese monk who was a Buddhist pilgrim to the site, first recorded their existence circa A.D. 632. Bamiyan became a major Buddhist center until Islam enveloped the region in the A.D. ninth century. The monumental Buddha described by Tsang "glittered with gold and precious ornaments." They must have been a sight to behold, with their shimmering gold gilt in the bright desert air, and could have been seen for many miles up and down the valley.

The Taliban finally gained complete control of the valley in 1998 and defaced the two statues in the head and the upper body with artillery fire, and in accordance with the belief that images of faces are forbidden in Islam. Shortly before this episode was to occur, and before the Taliban gained full control of the Bamiyan valley, the Taliban made it known that the massive Buddhas would be completely destroyed if they gained control of the valley. The Taliban then recanted due to the international outcry, and instead chose to deface the Buddhas, leaving a gaping hole where the heads had once been, but this still left open the possibility that the Taliban could change their mind at any time and decide to destroy all pre-Islamic archaeological sites along with their objects.

At this point in time, the UN and UNESCO still had some time to act, first by officially dropping the UNESCO accords relative to Afghanistan and the surrounding region, and then to begin involving some wealthy museums and other institutions in order to move forward and begin a process of evacuating as much ancient art as possible from the country.

The warning signs were clear and they came to a head when on February 26, 2001, an edict was announced by the Taliban's supreme leader, Mullah Muhammad Omar, that all pre-Islamic statues in the county were to be destroyed. This included the two Bamiyan statues, along with countless other works of art that were scattered around the country. The edict by the Mullah Muhammad Omar could have been a response to the U.N. sanctions implemented in January, following the Taliban's prior refusal to extradite the well-known Saudi terrorist, Osama bin Laden, whom US intelligence officers refer to as the "Ford Foundation of Terror," because of his multinational financial ability to fund his activities. In effect, this art destruction was probably triggered by the Taliban's hardened resistance to the UN and now, the Taliban have accelerated their art destruction and have engaged in what the UN now defines as *cultural terrorism.*

This scenario is a clear case how the antiquities trade could have been effective in saving and preserving at least some of the objects that were left intact in the country. The Taliban sent teams of men bent on destroying any object they could lay their hands on. These teams were known to have been active twenty-four in seven, and according to the Taliban's minister of Information and Culture, Qudratulla Jamal, who stated without any reservation:

"They are at work in the Kabul museum and in Ghazni, Heart, Jalalabad, and Kandahar provinces. These statues are no big issue, and they are only objects made of mud and stone."

Reports from some European news agencies revealed that many of the statues were reduced to small piles of rubble with picks and hammers, and that on March 12, tank and rocket fire totally obliterated the two Bamiyan Buddhist statues that survived the passing of Genghis Khan, Tamerlane, and even to some extent, the British army with their colonial field artillery.

The wholesale destruction of all pre-Islamic art by the hands of the Taliban also points to my assertion that the Taliban have an ancient mentality, and a modern organization like the UN and UNESCO are treated and seen by the Taliban as mere interlopers and infidels that can't be trusted or believed. This is a regime that fills an abandoned soccer stadium in Kabul nearly every day, so that the masses can witness the public execution of those poor souls, many of them women that were accused of crimes against the Taliban's definition of Islam. Depending on their crime against the state, they are callously shot in the back of the head, hanged, and even buried up to their necks and are then stoned to death. With this all under the eyes of the crowd that is in the stands enjoying refreshments, the stark reality to ancient Rome is not lost, with the arena serving as an instrument for the preservation of the state.

I also found it difficult to believe that the UN could think that economic sanctions would have some impact on the Taliban, as the sanctions impacted the people, rather than the Taliban regime that controls the food supply and every aspect of social life in the country. I found it even harder to accept that after the Taliban defaced the Bamiyan statues in 1998 that the UN really believed that the Taliban would not destroy every monument in the country along with an infinite number of ancient works of art. This art destruction falls in line with the Taliban restoration of the *khilaafa*, meaning caliphate, which would encompass the entire Muslim world.

Shortly before the destruction of the art began in early 2001, Afghan archaeologists in Kabul knew what the future held. They pleaded with Swiss architect Paul Bucherer-Dietschi, the founder of the Afghanistan Museum in Bubendorf, Switzerland, to remove what objects he could from the Kabul Museum for safekeeping in Switzerland. His response was the following seen in *Archaeology*, May/June 2002, page 22:

"I had to tell them I couldn't do it without the official agreement of UNESCO. Even if I had their agreement, I now doubt whether the Afghans would have managed to bypass al-Qaeda. But at the time, Rabbani, the recognized president of Afghanistan, gave written permission in May 2000 to bring materials here to Bubendorf and this was not acceptable to UNESCO. The president of a country is responsible for the belongings of his nation, and if his request is not accepted, I do not know what else can be done."

The apparent hypocrisy and utter failure of the UNESCO accords relative to Afghanistan is now clear enough, concerning the destruction of all pre-Islamic art within the country, and the question now becomes in the not-so-distant future, will these accords contribute towards locking objects in another country that are marked for wanton destruction?

The UN and UNESCO answer for this type of problem perhaps lies with the additions to the Geneva Conventions, in 1977 and 1997, that prohibit the callous and malicious destruction of cultural property in civil as well as international wars. The International War Crimes Tribunal is now forming charges against members of the former government of Yugoslavia for the destruction of cultural property, and labeling them as "war crimes," but these charges are really secondary when these same individuals are charged with genocide. It remains to be seen if the charges of cultural terrorism are filed against those that are responsible for these crimes in Afghanistan.

The immediate UN and UNESCO response to the Taliban edict was one of sheer panic and disbelief, but to their credit, United Nations Secretary General Kofi Annan hastily marshaled an "appeal for preservation" from about a dozen nations, including Pakistan which is the Taliban's closest, and perhaps, only true ally, although the Taliban government is also recognized by Saudi Arabia and the United Arab Emirates, the latter of which is a country that is a center of the unregulated *hawala* moneychanging and transfer system. Annan also traveled to Pakistan; in order to make his statement and firm up additional support in Pakistan. The head of UNESCO, Koichiro Matsuura, convened an emergency meeting of members of the Organization of the Islamic Conference in an effort to try to stop the destruction. He then dispatched special envoy, Pierre Lafrance, to Kandahar to plead for the Buddha's preservation.

The director of the Metropolitan Museum of Art in New York, Philippe de Montebello, boldly stepped forward and offered the following proposal:

"We deplore the destruction of major examples of the world's cultural heritage. We, the Metropolitan, would be prepared to come with experts at our own cost and, in collaboration with them, take pieces that are obviously portable and preserve them in the Met."

The officials at the Met probably knew what the situation was like in Afghanistan before the Taliban edict, which called for the destruction of the pre-Islamic ancient works of art, and they probably feared for the worst and were extremely frustrated that their hands were tied and that there was nothing that they, or any other public institution of the art world could do. The UNESCO accords politically prevented them, or at least held them back, from officially and publicly taking measures that could have saved many of the objects that were subsequently destroyed. The political mountain was too high to surmount, and of course, all of that crumbled as soon as the edict was announced and the destruction of the art began, and by then it was too late for many of the thousands of ancient works of art that were destroyed by the Taliban.

It would have been interesting to know what the position of the Archaeological Institute of America's (AIA) view of the Met would have been, if in fact, the Met or any other museum decided to move forward with a rescue plan, before the Taliban edict and the destruction of the art. This rescue plan would have run counter to the AIA position put forth by its president, Nancy Wilkie, who has stated the following in *Archaeology*, May/June 2001, p.6:

"Because much of the pillaging occurs to satisfy the lucrative illegal trade in antiquities, the AIA has supported requests to restrict the importation into the United States of artifacts from signatories to the 1970 UNESCO Convention on the Means of Prohibiting the Illicit Import, Export, and Transfer of Ownership of Cultural Property."

Perhaps more effective measures to save the art and the Buddhist monuments were taken on by the government of Japan, which unilaterally made it clear that they would cut off all aid to Afghanistan if the Buddhist statues were destroyed. Japan has a high number of Buddhists and the destruction of the Buddhist statues was not only repulsive to them, but it was also sacrilegious. A team from Japan was sent to Afghanistan with a letter from Foreign Minister Yohei Kono that urged the Taliban to seriously reconsider their demolition. Japan was one of the few countries to step forward and take concrete action, regarding the destruction of the monuments, and what separated their actions from that of the UN and UNESCO was that they were threatening to take action, rather than plead and beg the Taliban to reconsider the destruction. I think the Japanese should be highly credited for their actions and, in my opinion, possibly did the most of any country to try and save the Buddhist monuments.

My experience with many of the Japanese collectors that I have worked with is that they are very sensitive to the message that many ancient works of art convey to them. Many Japanese collectors have an inner sense of the aesthetic, and have a high level of appreciation for art that illustrates a great deal of eye appeal. Since many Japanese are Buddhists, they view much of the material that comprises a religious monument or statuette as living matter, and as such, these divine objects derive power from the earth and nature.

This process is a transmutation of power and life through the modification of form. Therefore, the mindset of the Japanese collector is one of refined taste and spiritual satisfaction, and many forms of Buddhist art is conceptualized as "living art" that is also spiritual, so for them, the destruction of the monuments by the Taliban is tantamount to murder.

In the end, the UN decided that they would not place any additional sanctions upon the Taliban and there would be no more reprisals, due primarily because of the Afghan people were, and are now, starving and freezing to death during the harsh winters. The UN basically cut bait and backed off the entire episode, and perhaps this was not a bad thing, considering the deplorable condition that the Afghan civilian population was, and is now, in. As far as I know, the UNESCO accords are still officially in place relative to Afghanistan and the surrounding region, and this sad state of affairs is even sadder, when one considers that there may still be some intact objects in Afghanistan. These objects may have been hidden by a few brave souls that are now looking for an avenue to get them out of the country, hoping perhaps to raise a pittance to feed their families.

A Japanese friend called me the other day and said in broken English: "Kevin, why did not anyone try save some of the Buddhist objects?"

I could only answer, "Politics and an antiquated international system of laws probably prevented that from happening. We can only hope that this sets an example in the future to allow for the free flow of objects so that that they may be saved."

I didn't hear an answer for a few seconds, and he simply said, "A pity." And then he quietly hung up the phone.

Author's Note: On the morning of September 11, 2001, agents of Osama bin Laden and/or members of his al-Qaeda organization, highjacked four United States flag carrier aircraft and committed the largest terrorist attack on U.S. soil in U.S. history, and the day before, the Northern Alliance's commander, Ahmad Shah Maksood, was mortally wounded in a bomb attack. The result was the complete destruction of the World Trade Center complex in New York City and severe damage to the Pentagon. Hundreds of innocent lives were lost and economic, social, and spiritual turmoil was the result. Although the above chapter was written before this dark period in our history, it was this author's hope that the publication of this work could have been completed prior to this heinous act, so that the readers could have some additional insights regarding the *ancient mentality* of the Taliban and other individuals such as Osama bin Laden who engage in world terrorism.

The dangers of this *ancient mentality* is now apparent as it rejects the modern concepts such as the separation of church and state, pluralism in government, and free market capitalism. It is a mentality that is determined, rather than one that is mad, and condemns the modern concepts of freedom of religion and western civilization as we know it. It is a mentality that pits the fabric of their society against the one of our own and where war is the answer and the preserver for their way of life, in contrast where peace is the core of our society.

It was, and is my opinion, that the Taliban attitude towards the United Nations and the western democratic nations, was hardened with the destruction of the Buddhist art within Afghanistan, and this act was not only a direct reflection of this *ancient mentality,* but it was also a *symbolic destruction* that revealed how reactionary the Taliban had become for the advancement of their cause. It may be that the Taliban's engagement in *cultural terrorism* buoyed others to further their terrorist activities in other countries, including the United States, and in addition to the incidents of the 1998 embassy bombings in east Africa and the U.S.S. *Cole* attack, this art destruction was perhaps a greater prelude of what was to come. It should be recognized that the destruction of the Buddhist art in Afghanistan was a *symbolic* one, along with the destruction of the World Trade Towers and the damage to the Pentagon, which together, represent the ultimate financial and military symbols of the United States.

Moreover, the *ancient mentality,* imprinted with the Hellenistic ideal of zealous devotion to the gods, defines a world where religion should reach beyond what is seen. The Taliban and especially Osama bin Laden have followed this thinking with their concept of *unlimited Islam,* which is global in scope. As the Hellenistic armies did twenty three hundred years ago in ancient Bactria, i.e., modern-day northern Afghanistan, with their spread of Greek Hellenistic culture, the Taliban and Osama bin Laden are now exporting their brand of Islam on a global scale, and as such, is the manifest destiny of the *ancient mentality.* One can argue if this *ancient mentality* is the root cause for a clash of cultures, but without question, the nature of our American democracy and our modern society has masked its existence, and the events of September 11 have made us all question the why behind the tragedy.

Our democracy is delicate, if not fragile, and as an American, it is my hope that this work may reveal some insights to what I have defined as an *ancient mentality*, so that it may give us some added strength in the years to come against the faceless war on terrorism and contribute to our understanding of a people that is still locked within an ancient world that few of us can know or even understand.

CHAPTER TWELVE

The Geneva Seizure

Giacomo Medici is a nice sort of guy with a friendly smile and an easygoing personality. He is somewhat stocky, with a dark complexion, halfway bald, and has a slight paunch, as many men in their mid-fifties have. He also had to use his reading glasses, as he viewed the latest Sotheby's *London Antiquities* catalog, which was the December 8, 1994 auction. The auction was being held in the tightly crammed Colonnade Galleries in Sotheby's aged building at 34-35 New Bond Street. There were a lot of familiar faces in attendance, including many New York and London dealers. Lot number 146 came up and it was a lovely Attic Red-Figure Lekythos, in the manner of the Berlin Painter, possibly by the Tithonos Painter, and it was dated circa 470 B.C. Approximately 13.5 inches tall, the piece was extremely elegant for an Attic *red-figure* vessel, and it was decorated with a splendid flying Nike that was seen in profile and appeared to be slightly floating in air. The art reminded me of the rare flying Nike that sometimes can be seen on the reverse of some Alexander the Great's gold coinage, notably the gold staters and distaters that were minted, circa 340 B.C. The flying Nike was depicted as a goddess, as the figure gave the illusion of defying gravity, and it was no wonder that the piece commanded an estimate of £15, 000-20,000 pounds, which in 1994 was about $25,000.00-$35,000.00.

Giacomo, seated directly in front of me, leaned over to the

gentleman to his immediate left and said, "Too much repaint, not so original but nice," he said with a friendly smile and a shrug with his head.

I couldn't help but overhear, and I thought he would be an interesting person to carry a conversation with after the auction. I continued to monitor the progress of the auction in hopes that I might be able to pick something off that was priced well. A few lots later, number 165 came up, which was also the last lot in the first session. Everyone, at this point in the auction, broke for lunch and some would return for the second session at 2:30 P.M. It was often during these lunch breaks, at the major sales, that a great deal of business would be discussed and many pieces would trade hands. I wanted to speak more with the man in front of me, but he got a good start and left a few lots before the end of the first session. I recalled that he appeared to be somewhat in a hurry, which was not unusual, for he was probably off for an important lunch meeting.

I broke for my lunch appointment, and made my way to Spink & Son Ltd. on 5, 6, & 7 King Street to view some ancient coins that John Pett had to offer. I was to learn later that the man seated in front of me was none other than Giacomo Medici, who was known in London as an avid collector who owned many pieces and often bought and sold, at both Sotheby's and Christie's in London and New York.

I never was able to connect with Giacomo Medici, because only a few months later, he was hounded in Italy by the investigative reporter Peter Watson, who was in the process of researching material for his soon-to-be published *Sotheby's Inside Story* (London, Bloomsbury Publishing Plc, 1997). At this point, Giacomo became difficult to reach and a few years later, on January 21, 1997, the Italians, in combination with Swiss authorities, raided his private storage facility at the Geneva Freeport in Geneva, Switzerland. His four rented units were broken into without any warning and their contents were quickly photographed and possibly some of the contents, if not all, were carted away in trucks by a wide array of Swiss and Italian bureaucrats that were complemented with men that were armed with heavy automatic weapons. For those of us in the trade, this episode would come to be known as the *Geneva Seizure*.

The Swiss magistrate, Jean-Pierre Trembley, approved a search warrant that enabled the authorities to go into the Geneva Freeport, load everything up, and truck it to an undisclosed location. In the process, it is unknown how many objects were shipped away, and/or how many objects remain sequestered at the Freeport, and if any of the pieces were damaged and broken. From personal experience in packing and shipping delicate ceramics, they have to be handled with a great deal of care, including wrapping them in bubble wrap, etc. There were many delicate pieces in Medici's collection that did require special handling, and I think it is very likely that there was some damage and breaks to a number of the pieces, especially if they were shipped from point "A" to point "C," and possibly back again. If there was some damage incurred to the pieces, this might also affect the monetary value of the collection, as intact mint quality pieces tend to command higher prices in Europe, in contrast to the U.S. market.

Giacomo Medici currently has filed a lawsuit against the Italian government for the return of his objects, and if he wins his case, the condition of the collection may be significant if there is a settlement. A Geneva court has revoked Jean-Pierre Trembley's assertion that the objects should be returned to Italy and has stated that the provenance of the artifacts had to be proven before they could be returned. Italy has filed an appeal relative to the Geneva court's ruling and Switzerland's Federal Court will hear the case. To date, Medici has not been formally charged with any crime, and as far as I am aware, there are no additional formal charges being filed against him in the near future.

His case, documented by Peter Watson in his book *Sotheby's Inside Story,* was touched upon in an entire chapter titled, "The Apulian Vases." The crux of Watson's story paints Medici as a smuggling kingpin who for years plundered southern Italy's tombs for ancient Greek Apulian ceramics. Watson contended, through several clandestine investigations, that Medici was responsible for supplying the auction houses in London, notably Sotheby's, with an unlimited number of pieces, and in order to do so, smuggled them from Italy with the knowledge of Sotheby's and several of their employees in London.

Watson was able to base his case, relative to Sotheby's involvement, on internal documents, dated from 1975 through 1989, that were spirited out of Sotheby's by one of its former employees, a James Hodges, who on December 17, 1991, was convicted in Knightsbridge Crown Court of stealing an antique helmet and vase from Sotheby's, along with one charge of forgery and false accounting. Hodges was sentenced by Judge Lloyd to nine months imprisonment and served his time at Ford Open Prison, near Arundel in Sussex. Hodges was working under Felicity Nicholson, who as department head of antiquities at Sotheby's in London, made all the decisions as to what pieces would be consigned to auctions, along with their suggested estimates and reserves. In this capacity, Nickolson's true power was really who she chose to do business with, and perhaps she did work with her favorites and offered them reduced commissions, but on the face of it, this is not a crime, and in the auction art world, this is actually good business. Nickolson would be assured in the future that she would be able to obtain fine pieces for subsequent auctions, and if one particular dealer like Medici was able to net her good pieces that he consigned as the owner, then who can blame her for working with him? In addition and perhaps more telling, he was a heavy *buyer* and one of her best clients.

One thing Watson did not make clear in his book, *Sotheby's Inside Story*, was that Medici was not only a dealer, but more importantly, he was a collector and often purchased objects worldwide from many auctions, including Sotheby's. Medici also dealt with other dealers and collectors, and was well known in the London market to frequently trade pieces that he acquired in London, for additional pieces in London and New York. Medici would also warehouse these pieces in Geneva and consummate a sale or a trade, sometimes years after he purchased a particular piece.

Photographs taken of his objects during the seizure clearly show auction identification tags that are attached to the pieces. These tags often illustrate the name of the auction company, with a corporate logo on one side, and the other, the auction and lot number. Did Watson miss the auction tags seen in the seizure photographs? One of the seizure photographs published in his book, *Sotheby's Inside Story,* clearly shows four auction tags that are attached to four of the ten objects that are fully seen in the photo. (See the three *Geneva Seizure* photos illustrated in *Sotheby's Inside Story* after page 120. Note the bottom photo fully illustrating the ten objects, with two objects on the top shelf and two objects on the bottom shelf with auction identification tags. The bronze running man on the top shelf with the auction identification tag is the same object seen in *Sotheby's, Antiquities—The Property of the Thetis Foundation and Other Owners*, London, May 23, 1991, page no. 47, lot no. 77. This piece is also published in J. Zimmermann, *Collection de la Foundation Thetis*, Catalog of an exhibition held at the Musee d'art et d'histoire, Geneva, 1987, page 39, no. 74. The piece is described as an East Greek Bronze Figure of a Running Hero, circa 540-530 B.C.)

Did Hodges, or anyone else for that manner, point these auction identification tags out to Watson and identify them as such? Did Watson have a clear understanding that many of Medici's objects were legally purchased in multiple auctions worldwide? Why would Watson remotely consider publishing any of the Geneva Freeport photos if he realized that they illustrated objects that had auction identification tags?

Watson failed to take these points into account in his book and does not mention the above facts anywhere in the text, and perhaps his true failing is that he is a journalist looking into the trade, rather than a journalist that was an integral part of the trade, and if this were true to some extent, he would have known Medici to be both a dealer and a collector. This is important, in that, Medici's role as both a dealer and a collector is a fact that may help define and contribute towards addressing the provenance of many of the pieces found in the Geneva Freeport. Could it be that this critical information was known to Hodges and was withheld, or was simply omitted from Watson's investigation?

Another question that Watson never addressed was why did Medici use the Geneva Freeport to store his collection? The first point that may go far in addressing this question is that the Geneva Freeport is exactly that-a free port. At least that is how it is represented to its clients who lease their storage facilities. The Freeport is a transshipment facility that is free from Swiss sovereignty and taxes, and this was the impression I got when I visited the facility in 1997. A guard who spoke English explained that the facility was not a part of Swiss soil, and therefore, the Swiss have no legal and sovereign standing to enter the Freeport at any time, but I was later able to learn from a Freeport representative that apparently the Swiss authorities can in fact enter the Geneva Freeport facility, as the facility does fall under Swiss jurisdiction, but the goods themselves do not, as they are considered to be in transit and are therefore free of duty and/or tax.

My own impression of the Freeport's security was that it was not unlike the security found in any governmental embassy found throughout the world. Guards would extensively check people in and out, as well as any shipments that enter and leave the facility, and security cameras monitor all activity. It would be interesting to know if Medici's attorneys examined the fine legal print regarding its operating charter and what was disclosed in his leasing contract, relative to any guarantees that the Freeport may have made towards safeguarding his property and the overall security of the facility. Obviously, a Swiss magistrate breached the security of the Geneva Freeport facility and one adept European dealer added the following comment:

"A Swiss magistrate with the stroke of a pin was able to breach the security of the Geneva Freeport, with the seizure of tax-free goods, and one has to wonder if the Swiss banking system is subject to the same scrutiny and legal maneuvering."

This brings another question to mind and that is—did the Swiss violate any of their own neutrality laws in seizing the goods of Giacomo Medici that were technically in transit at the Geneva Freeport? Did the Swiss Magistrate, Jean-Pierre Trembley, have the power to supersede Swiss federal neutrality law by enabling the Geneva Seizure to take place? In addition, Switzerland is currently not a member of the European Union (EU), unlike Italy that is, and does this cast another legal wrinkle on this whole affair?

What is perhaps the most shocking element of the *Geneva Seizure* is that the Italian government confiscated Medici's entire collection as property of the Italian state. Meaning that, according to the Italians, they were enforcing their Law for the Protection of Cultural Properties, No. 1089, which took effect under Mussolini in 1939 and it obliges the state to preserve and protect cultural objects of major importance. This law also allows the state to control the movement of significant objects in the possession of Italian private citizens by "listing" the objects together with the name and address of the owner, and to further complicate the private ownership of antiquities by Italian private citizens, a recent decision by the Italian Supreme Court declares that any individual who is found in possession of archaeological objects must be able to prove that they come from collections formed before 1909, and the lack of adequate documentation implies illegal provenance and will result in the confiscation of the object. In addition, Article 44 of law No. 1089 declares that all found objects belong to the state and all "listed" objects cannot be exported.

In Medici's case, the Italian authorities asserted that all of his pieces originated from Italian soil and their ownership reverts back to the Italian government, and this contention by the Italian government runs contrary to English common property law and the concept of private property law. English common property law is not only a pillar upon which our society is based in the free world, but it is also the centerpiece for our capitalist form of government. Even the Italians might consider, along with the officials in other countries that put a rubber stamp on these raiding parties, what's next to be nationalized and what personal freedoms and property will be "listed" in the near future?

The heart of this whole episode may lie in the very nature of the pieces themselves. Frederick Schultz, a New York gallery owner by that name, and acting president of the NADAOP (National Association of Dealers in Ancient, Oriental and Primitive Art), was able to examine photographs of the pieces that were seized, which are also published on the Internet at: http://www.archaeology.org/online/features/geneva/index.html.

There are also individual pieces that are seen at the Italian *Carabinieri* web site: http://www.carabinieri.it/tpa/tpa.asp.

Schultz was also able to note that many of Medici's pieces were purchased at past auctions, based on what the photographs of the seized pieces were able to show, relative to their attached auction identification tags, and the fact that the objects themselves visually match the photos seen in many different auction catalogs. Schultz was further able to identify and analyze the objects themselves and concluded that most of the objects of possible Italic origin were from old bona fide collections, this in addition to the fact that a great number of the objects were of non-Italic origin, and were produced by cultures that dwelled outside the confines of the modern state of Italy. These cultures included Egyptian, Urartu (Near Eastern), Cypriot, Celtic (Britain and northern Europe), and Greek (Greece, Turkey, and Asia Minor). (See the Appendix with commentary from Schultz regarding the cultural origin of the objects photographed in the *Geneva Seizure*.)

Here again, Watson failed to take this into account and apparently took at face value what General Conforti, the head of the art squad of the Italian *Carabinieri,* had to say, or neglected to say about the nature and/or cultural origin of the pieces themselves. Watson elaborates on a brief description given to him by General Conforti concerning the pieces, seen on page 276 of his book *Sotheby's Inside Story:*

"General Conforti (he had been promoted in the New Year from colonel) told us that these warehouses contained 10,000 'finely made' antiquities from sites all over Italy. They were of Etruscan, Roman, Apulian and Campanian origin, and valued at 50 miliard lire or £25 million (English pounds). This was an enormous sum-far greater than we had expected-and possibly the largest and most valuable seizure of antiquities ever made."

This description of the seized objects describes Conforti's definition of the number of seized objects and their perceived value, rather than the number of commercial grade objects and their cultural description/attribution. In General Conforti's official statement, which was also published in Watson's book on page 276-277, he states that:

"In view of their large number and their historical importance, once they are back in Italy these objects, which have already been catalogued by the representative of the Archaeological Superintendent for Southern Etruria, could give rise to the establishment of a new archaeological museum."

Watson seems to agree with the phrase, "*once they are back in Italy these objects,*" that is seen in General Conforti's official statement. The question may be open as to whether many of the objects of the *Geneva Seizure* were ever in Italy in the first place, and this is further supported by Frederick Schultz, who concluded the following in a letter, also seen on the Internet at the site noted above, that is addressed to the publishers of the photographs of the seized pieces-Andrew Slayman and *Archaeology* (See Appendix):

"After reading Peter Watson's *Sotheby's: The Inside Story* and myriad subsequent magazine articles about the renowned antiquities kingpin, Giacomo Medici, I was thrilled to be able to see the images posted on your website 'Geneva Seizure,' which purports to display '10,000 artifacts, most of them probably smuggled from Italy.' Instead of proving that Mr. Medici is the secret smuggling connection from Italy, however, your website proved exactly the opposite, and proved it beyond a shadow of a doubt. With the exception of the Ostia column capitals, every object of possible Italian provenience comes from a bona fide old collection. My comments refer to the photos as numbered on the website."

Schultz responded to Andrew Slayman and the *Archaeology* Internet site, in part, because he was then the acting president of the NADAOPA, and he felt that the well-publicized *Geneva Seizure* needed a response from the NADAOPA, at least this is what he indicated to me when I met with him in October of 2001. A simplified summation of their principles is seen in their membership directory, which is designed as a three-part brochure. The following is seen on the inside front page:

"The National Association of Dealers in Ancient, Oriental and Primitive Art was founded as a not-for-profit organization in 1975. The association was instrumental in drafting cultural property legislation pursuant to the UNESCO Convention, which has permitted museums and private collectors to continue acquiring antiquities, tribal and Asian works of art. We believe that sensible antiquities laws and realistic collecting guidelines are essential to the free and open worldwide movement of cultural properties. Our members are committed to connoisseurship, scholarship and the highest ethical standards."

Schultz also noted that the number "10,000 artifacts" defined by General Conforti and mentioned by Watson in Sotheby's Inside Story, is a misnomer, because this number probably included objects that had little or no commercial value and were made up of fragments and pieces of bronze, glass, and terracotta.

Schultz, based on his examination of the seizure photographs, concluded that there were approximately 600 to 900 commercial grade objects and Medici himself maintains that there were approximately 200 to 300 commercial grade objects taken, and that they were certainly worth far less that the purported value of £25 million (English pounds). (See the Appendix with Giacomo Medici's letter and his response to Andrew Slayman and *Archaeology*.)

My own research of the seizure photographs revealed approximately 550 intact objects that appeared to be of commercial grade. Given the fact that the published seizure photos I examined may not be complete, this may throw the numbers off, but the photos I did examine certainly did not reveal "10,000 artifacts" of any kind that were completely intact, and there definitely were not anywhere near "10,000 artifacts" that appeared to be commercial grade. The photos also appeared to represent four separate rooms or storage units, as a few of the photos showed the length of the rooms with three walls seen within the photos. This allowed me to piece together the photos, with their displayed objects room by room.

Regarding the value of the objects, I was able to come up with an average value per piece that was derived from past auction sales at Sotheby's in New York. I used the New York sales from 1995 to 2000, because the sales are in dollars; the New York market for antiquities tends to be slightly stronger than the London market, and the *Geneva Seizure* was in January of 1997 and the New York auction values bracket this date. The prices realized in New York also tend to reflect a stronger value across the board for the various cultures. I found from 1995 to 2000, there was a total of ten separate auctions, as Sotheby's held two major antiquities sales per year in New York. The pieces with realized prices-in other words, pieces that sold at auction totaled approximately 1,800. The total gross value of the sold pieces realized approximately $10 million for all five years, and this value included the buyer's premium, which is a fifteen percent commission that is paid to the auction house.

I then took this value, minus the sales commission, and divided it by the number of pieces that were sold by Sotheby's (1,800) and this yielded an average value of $4,722.00 per piece. I then multiplied this average value per piece against the numbers of pieces that Schultz estimated were of commercial grade, and that amounted to approximately 600 to 900 objects. This gave me an average value of approximately $2,833,200.00 to $4,249,800.00 dollars, and it's probable that this figure is unrealistic, as a great majority of the pieces seen in the photos are of poor quality and are minor ($300.00-$900.00 dollars in value) to midrange pieces ($1,000.00-$3,000.00 dollars in value).

If one plugged my number of approximately 550 objects into the equation, the average value of the *Geneva Seizure* is approximately $2,597,100.00, and given this mathematical scenario is probably not perfectly accurate and that this figure is only an estimate, it does reveal some idea as to what the true market value of the seized objects may actually be worth and is based on realized prices in the market, rather than unfounded speculation. One should note that I used the New York realized values, as opposed to the London realized values, and that I did not account for the numerous minor to midrange pieces that were included in the equation that are factored as having a *higher* average value per piece, which was an estimated average value of $4,722.00 per piece. Either one of the above factors plugged into the equation, would have yielded a *lower* estimated total value for the seized pieces. My conservative average value of the *Geneva Seizure,* approximately $2,597,100.00, may be greater than the actual worth of the collection and yet this value, based on the 550 objects that I identified, is a far cry from the values quoted by General Conforti and Peter Watson.

After Watson's book was published and distributed in Europe, coincidentally in time for the March 8, 1997 European Fine Art Fair in Maastricht, The Netherlands, the AIDAA responded with Schultz's findings via the Internet and other members of the organization followed suit. One prominent member, the wily Dr. Jerry M. Eisenberg, founder, editor-in-chief, and publisher of *Minerva*, responded through a series of articles in *Minerva* in 1997. The following was seen in the news section of the November/December issue of *Minerva*, page 6, titled "The Antiquities Trade Attacked in the Times: A Further Commentary on the Ancient Art Market":

"The writer wrote in the September/October issue of *Minerva* ('Enough Is Enough, Lord Renfrew!') of his concerns about extreme attacks being made on the antiquities trade by Lord Renfrew, Disney Professor of Archaeology at Cambridge University, and Professor Ricardo J. Elia of Boston University, who in their wildly exaggerated assertions rank the antiquity dealer as second only to the drugs smuggler or illegal arms dealer by their 'trafficking in illegal antiquities.' The writer hopes that his commentary in *Minerva* helped to lay to rest these nonsensical claims. He also wishes to thank the many readers who wrote and telephoned to convey their agreement with his statements—including a good number of academics.

Now Peter Watson, the author of the recent *Sotheby's Inside Story*, has written a two-part article in *The Times* of London, August 14-15, stating that up to ninety percent of the antiquities sold in the London auction market have no provenance, based on figures supplied by Drs. David Gill and Christopher Chippindale. Mr. Watson then proceeds to claim that 'very few antiquities have ever been in an old collection or someone's attic. Instead, most objects without a history may have been illegally excavated and smuggled—and fairly recently at that.' After relating the case of an ancient vase being consigned by an agent of a known participant in the illegal antiquities trade in Italy and then being sold to a noted collector, and pointing out the possibility of improper provenances of three antiquities, he states that: 'We are left, therefore, with the inescapable conclusion that many modern collections are, for the most part, made up of valuable objects that have been illegally excavated, smuggled out of their country of origin, often then bought at auction, with labels attached that may well be archaeologically meaningless.'

It is indeed surprising that Mr. Watson has the clairvoyance to make this assumption! If he had taken the time to examine some of the hundreds of auctions of antiquities conducted in the nineteenth century and the first half of the twentieth century he would be aware that a very small percentage of antiquities sold then bore a provenance. The writer would be more than pleased to point out some of the dozens of major auctions in which tens of thousands of legally acquired but unprovenanced pieces were sold. There are also countless thousands of originally provenanced objects, which have lost their labels and can only sometimes be identified by the style of labeling on the object or the type of base used. Huge collections, for example, of Egyptian objects were sold in the 1910s and 1920s by such prominent enthusiasts as Lady Meux, F.G. Hilton Price, the Reverend W. MacGregor (a nine-day sale!)—and the great majority of these had no provenance, and following the sales the attribution to the specific collection was also often lost. The writer in the 1950s and 1960s brought out many thousands of antiquities from Egypt, all legally purchased and exported with official museum permits (at that time a number of dealers were licensed by the government for the sale of antiquities)—but he can testify that a good deal more than ninety percent had no provenance. In 1960 he acquired 2,740 Egyptian scarabs from the Reverend Nash collection through Spink and Son in London. All were dispersed in 1965, entering the collections of many private individuals, and one may speculate as to how many still bear their provenance."

Dr. Eisenberg's brief historical overview concerning the provenance of antiquities seems to strengthen Medici's argument for the return of his objects. In all fairness to Watson, Watson could be right to some degree that Medici did engage in smuggling antiquities out of Italy and was selling them into the international market, with some of them being consigned to auction at Sotheby's. Watson's documents leave a great deal of questions because they only reveal part of the picture, with one looking at documents "A" and "C," and assuming what document "B" had to reveal. Watson, to his credit, even admits this omission and weakness with his documents, and his conclusions are compelling and seem logical, but as far as examining the provenance of the objects legally purchased by Medici at auction and defining the cultures that originally produced the objects that were seized in the Geneva Freeport, he perhaps missed the mark.

This is significant, because the numbers and the dollar amounts of the seized pieces in the Geneva *Seizure* were built into a dialog that has been used to attack the trade. Ricardo Elia's, the AIA's (Archaeological Institute of America) Vice President for Professional Responsibilities, recent testimony before the Cultural Property Advisory Committee (CPAC) stated that during the years 1980-1992, more than 4,000 Apulian red-figure vases were offered for sale, none of which were recorded in private collections or belonging to a museum, and referred to the recent arrest of individuals involved with looting in Italy and involving more than 30,000 antiquities.

The question is again open as to how Elia came up with his numbers and did he incorporate the numbers referred to by General Conforti in the Geneva seizure, i.e., the "10,000 artifacts" number?

At the time of Elia's testimony before the Cultural Property Advisory Committee (CPAC), which was drafted under the 1983 Cultural Property Implementation Act (CPIA), the committee was hearing evidence and testimony from several individuals as to whether they should recommend a bilateral agreement between the US and Italy to restrict the import of antiquities of Italic origin into the United States. The Cultural Property Advisory Committee (CPAC) was created as a body by Congress to make recommendations to the U.S. State Department and in short, the CPAC committee is a legislative body that forms U.S. foreign policy. This U.S. foreign policy is realized in the formation and adoption of bilateral agreements between the US and foreign countries regarding the restriction of importing certain types of ethnographic or archaeological material from within their borders. The CPIA legislation that created CPAC was to insure a balance of interests from dealers, collectors, museums, archaeologists, and those nations concerned about looting. A nation seeking U.S. import restrictions for antiquities must first draft a petition stating the reasons for the request and must meet certain criteria, including identifying categories of endangered objects in combination with specific sites that are endangered by looters. CPAC, as of this writing, is currently chaired by Maria Kouroupas and determines which petitions are rejected, accepted, or amended. It's interesting to note that not a single petition in the 18-year history of CPAC has ever been rejected outright. Moreover, the original CPIA legislation drafted by Congress was to ensure a broad interest of the American people by mandating that the body of CPAC be composed of eleven members—three from the archaeological community, three from the art trade, three reflecting the public interest, and two associated with museums. It's also interesting to note, as of this writing, that the only current member of CPAC that is from the art trade is Kate Fitz Gibbon, owner of the Anahita Gallery in Santa Fe, New Mexico, who markets some Asian antiques and photographs.

The reality is that there is no true specialist from the art trade with a great deal of expertise relative to classical and pre-Columbian antiquities that is currently a member of CPAC, and perhaps this is no accident as there are strict State Department conflict-of-interest regulations that may be partly responsible for keeping dealers from becoming involved with CPAC. It's also no secret that many involved in the antiquities trade regard these bilateral agreements as sort of a diplomatic "chit" for the U.S. State Department, in other words, we'll support you with your request for import restrictions, and in return, you don't give us any trouble relative to our U.S. air bases in your country in addition to your military and political support.

As a result of the hearings regarding the Italian petition, a five-year bilateral agreement was adopted and became effective on January 23, 2001. Was the testimony at these hearings skewed with numbers that were, in part, derived from the Geneva seizure? Did anyone ask in the hearings about the validity of the numbers of antiquities involved and the true scale of the smuggling of objects from Italy? With the implementation of the bilateral agreement, is this an avenue for Italy to gain money from the UN and UNESCO to fight an antiquities trade that may not really be as grand as it was claimed to be in the hearings, and if so, how much money was allocated to the Italian government?

In addressing the first question, it's really hard to say. Anyone can juggle numbers to fit a picture in a myriad of ways, and this is my point—*there is an inherent weakness of using numbers of objects to prove a point, which is used as a barometer to gauge the scale of a problem, such as the looting and smuggling of archaeological material from Italy.* The definition of the objects themselves may not be taken into account, and it's easy to insert objects that have no commercial value, and in some cases may even be fragments and parts of a whole object.

In addressing the second question, the answer is probably no, because when one looks at the individuals that are on the Cultural Property Advisory Committee (CPAC), there is not one member that is a major dealer or an active member of the trade with a great deal of expertise. This opens the debate field to questions that may favor the anti-trade components that gave their testimony.

In addressing the third question, the bilateral agreement itself is somewhat ambiguous and U.S. Customs has said that they will handle each case on a case-by-case basis. Some types of archaeological material are excluded and other types are not. However, what is not ambiguous is that Italy now has new helicopters to patrol their archeological sites, including the new Agusta-Bell 206 and 412, along with military hardware such as night vision glasses that detect body heat in the dark of night. This new hardware is seen every month in *Il Carabiniere* magazine and the April 2002 issue features one of their new helicopters with all its new high-tech gear on the front cover.

The *Carabinieri* have transformed themselves into a modern military operation complete with heavy automatic weapons. This takes money and lots of it.

In Bari, which is a town in Apulia, everyone there is aware of the new high-tech helicopters manned by heavily armed men with itchy trigger fingers, but what about the tourists, could they be at times in the crossfire? What about the rumored random hotel and auto searches now taking place in Tuscany for Etruscan antiquities, especially with men armed with heavy automatic weapons? What about Italy's probable recent high-tech war on the trade with its monitoring and gathering information of Internet sites, including the names of people selling antiquities worldwide? Is UNESCO financing a high-tech operation of this sort and if so, how is this information used? Are known dealers and collectors identified on the Internet subject to searches if they enter the country?

There are numerous questions as to how Italy has allocated any funds that UNESCO may have granted them to use as they see fit. The Italians have mounted a diplomatic campaign to extend the time that they can hold the objects taken in the *Geneva Seizure*. Only time can tell, in Swiss Federal Court, whether Medici gets his objects back in one piece or not, and the outcome may have important implications for the trade. The *Geneva Seizure* may turn out to be an unfortunate episode for everyone involved, even for the Italians who initially had the most to gain.

CHAPTER THIRTEEN

The Steinhardt Affair

In 1991, Michael H. Steinhardt's first glimpse of the piece made his heart beat just a little faster and at that moment, it captured his soul. Steinhardt, a Wall Street financier and retired hedge fund manager, is one of a myriad of eccentric collectors in New York City that have a passion for ancient Greek antiquities. If the piece was exceptional, and if the piece happened to exceed his discerning expectations, he would generally pay a fair price. The price Steinhardt agreed to pay for this piece was in excess of $1 million, so not only were his expectations overwhelmed, the raw beauty of the vessel commanded his reality. In his mind, the money didn't really matter. Never mind the 1.2-million-dollar purchase price; he only wanted to posses an antiquity that would only come to a collector once in a lifetime, and for Michael Steinhardt—this was his *Maltese Falcon.*

The piece that ruled his world was an exquisite gold bowl that was about eight inches in diameter, otherwise known as a gold *phiale mesomphalos,* which was fashioned from one solid sheet of gold, circa 360-280 B.C. The vessel shimmered with a bright brilliance as one moved it with the light, and no wonder, for this extremely rare vessel is nearly 98 percent pure gold. The balance of the piece is composed of several base metals, the majority being copper and tin, and this lends credence to its authenticity due to the fact that mining methods in the

Classical period (circa 480-336 B.C.) did not completely refine trace amounts of impurities from the metal.

The piece was then beaten into its form, hand-etched, and detailed to minute perfection. The inside center displayed a raised circular roundel, known as an *omphalos*, which in the ancient Greek mind represented the center of the world. The ancient Greeks regarded the sacred site of Delphi in a similar context, and regarded it as the sacred center of the world, as Delphi enshrined the sacred half-egg stone known as the *omphalos* which in Greek means "navel." This omphalos, within Steinhardt's golden vessel, made it no doubt that it was a votive object, and was probably created for use and/or as an offering in a Greek temple. In antiquity, this type of vessel became the Greek libation vessel "par excellence" and was already in common use as a sacrificial vessel in Greece during the seventh century B.C. This type of shallow bowl, with a flat bottom, had no handles, and the central boss (omphalos) was usually punched up on the inside from the bottom, which served as a finger grip when pouring or drinking libations.

It's probable that the design of this type of vessel was first developed in central Asia, with several types attributed to the Achaemenid Empire that spanned modern-day Iran and Iraq. In time, the type-and more importantly-the intricate design of the vessel filtered into Greece during the *orientalising* phase of Greek art, which is described by art historians as a period that centered from the eighth through the seventh centuries B.C. This period was also the phase when ancient Greece first began to emerge from the collapse of the earlier Mycenaean civilization, circa 1100 B.C. The Mycenaean civilization existed throughout the Mediterranean during what historians refer to as the heroic age of Greece, when Mycenae under King Agamemnon was the dominant power and when the fabled Trojan expedition took place. The contact between Asia and mainland Greece during this period is well documented and it's possible that the design of the gold phiale first appeared in

Greece during the heroic age of Greece and further developed during the later orientalising phase of Greek art.

The votive nature of this stunning vessel is further emphasized with three rows of concentric rings of 36 acorns that diminish in size towards the center, and the spaces between the acorns are filled with minute ornament and motifs that are based upon palmate designs. The alternating acorns and bees, seen on the outer ring of the vessel, is symbolic of the earth's "victual in plenty," as described by the Greek poet Hesiod. Acorns and bees were also sacred to Zeus, and many religious centers throughout ancient Greece had oak groves that even today are seen running throughout the ruins. The most prominent sacred site that emphasized the oak tree is the oracle at Dodona, where many oak trees were planted so that visiting pilgrims could make an offering in their branches while visiting the oracle.

As one looks towards the center of the vessel, there is a detailed palmate band that runs between the omphalos and a single inner ring of beechnuts, which is a third symbol that alludes to the sacred nature of this gold phiale mesomphalos. The palmate band is a standard design that is found as an architectural element seen on many Greek temples, which is usually seen in the entablature of the structure. In addition, the palmate design is also seen on many Greek Attic pottery vessels during the fifth and fourth century B.C.

The details and votive design of the vessel did not escape the sharp eye of Michael Steinhardt; he instantly knew the secular nature of the piece and its artistic significance, as it was fashioned in the purest gold that the ancient artist could obtain and the workmanship was of the highest skill for the period. A few words punched below the rim, record the dedication to the gods by the demarch Achyris and its weight as 115 gold staters. The gold content alone, relative to the purchasing power in antiquity, made this a votive piece that was intended only for the gods, and Steinhardt had no difficulty in recognizing the importance of the vessel. Perhaps entering his mind was the analogous piece that is now in the Metropolitan Museum in New York, which was acquired circa 1962 from Robert E. Hecht, Jr. The design of this piece is nearly identical in form, and only a few other examples of this type are found in other private collections and museums worldwide. These gold vessels could only be found in a sacred shrine or temple, and may have been created solely as a dedication offering.

Perhaps a more telling element, relative to this type of vessel, was the mindset of the artist during the late classical period, circa 350 B.C. During the classical period, the ancient Greek culture was embedded with an obsession with the will of the gods and man's interrelationship with them, and consequently, the prevailing Greek thinking was universally frozen in a conviction that man wasn't worthy of possessing a beautiful piece such as this. The piece was probably created circa fourth-third century B.C., shortly before or after the subsequent Hellenistic period began, circa 336 B.C., and this latter period saw the development of man first placing his own portrait on coinage that in the earlier Classical period was reserved for the images of only the gods.

In the Hellenistic period, man had become decadent in many respects, so the votive pieces created in the prior Classical period had more religious significance, and the artist did his utmost to create a vessel that was pure perfection, and as such, was reserved only for the gods.

Steinhardt was an advanced enough collector to know all of this and there was no escape for him not to purchase the piece. Steinhardt may have also been aware that the artists who created these gold vessels were of the highest caliber and could have traveled from anywhere in the ancient Greek world, especially if the commission was great enough. In the fourth to the third century B.C., there were many artists who engraved coin dies that are known to have traveled great distances to produce a set of dies for a particular city or ruler. These artists were proud of their work, and in many cases they actually signed their dies with initials from their name or completely spelled out their name on a flat section of the flan. It's probable that many of the artists that produced coin dies also produced votive vessels fashioned from precious metals, in part, because they had access to precious metals and were skilled with engraving, casting, and forging the metal. An important votive vessel such as a gold phiale mesomphalos could have been produced where the artist lived and was later exported for trade, or the artist traveled to where the commission originated. In any case, the few facts that would perhaps help answer the question as to where an important gold vessel such as this might have been produced, would be the artistic style of the vessel, the period it was produced, and the metal content of the piece.

Steinhardt was in a position of wealth to entrust others to make things happen for him and the man he trusted was Robert Haber. Haber, a well-heeled antiquities dealer in New York, has his gallery at 16 West 23rd Street. Over the years, Haber gained a solid reputation in handling rare and expensive classical antiquities and worked with many distinguished collectors and museums. Always sporting a smart gold tie with a blue sport coat, Haber cut a refined image of knowledge and dependability, but perhaps due to circumstances beyond his control and events unknown to him, his marketing of the gold phiale mesomphalos went awry.

Haber first got wind of the piece from London dealer, William Veres, who operated a small shop at Lennox in the Mews off Davies Street near Oxford and New Bond Streets. Lennox is a mixed conglomeration of antique shops that are crammed together in an old converted red brick warehouse. Veres, who always seemed to clinch many a deal at his shop, was able to net the gold *phiale* from an Italian collector and dealer, a Vincenzo Cammarata who has a villa near Catania, Sicily. The locals know this Cammarata as "Il Barone," who was often seen traveling on his motorcycle in and out of the country roads. Always wearing his flamboyant leather hat while openly trading in antiquities, he fostered an Indiana Jones sort of image that was popular with many of the locals. Low key he was not, but perhaps an explanation for his open and flamboyant style of doing business was that he had many political and other shadowy contacts that seemed to shield him from any foreseeable problems with the local *Carabinieri;* at least that was the perception that many locals had of this individual.

Cammarata shopped the gold phiale in Italy until Giacomo Manganaro, 71, a professor of ancient history at the University of Catania, gave the piece an apparent nod of approval (circa 1988) and then, Cammarata traded the piece to Veres for artworks estimated to be worth approximately $90,000.00; at least this was the value that Cammarata later stated to Italian authorities. Court records also revealed that Cammarata claimed he traded art pieces for the gold phiale in 1980 with a Sicilian named Vincenzo Pappalardo, and before 1980, it is unclear as to exactly where the gold phiale originated; but what is clear, is that Cammarata was a student of Manganaro at the University of Catania and knew him for quite some time. It's important to realize that exactly how the pie was divided up, and what all of the various players netted for this deal is all open to speculation, but there is a wrinkle to the deal that no one has elaborated on, and that it was possible that Veres initially took a gamble on the piece and assumed it to be a fake prior to his controlling the piece, and perhaps Cammarata and Manganaro considered it a fake as well in the early stages of the deal.

Once the authenticity of the vessel was later established, apparently by the Metropolitan Museum in New York, a fair deal between all of the parties was probably negotiated, and this was in the best interests of both Haber and Veres, as Haber and Veres did not want the deal to later blow up in their faces. Both men were experienced in handling big deals and both men knew how to seal a deal like this, and this includes sharing the wealth in a fair and equitable manner. In this regard, this would insure that they would get additional pieces in the future and would avoid any other problems that would come up at a later date.

I also learned from several of their business associates that they both had consummated much bigger deals in the past and are regarded as reputable dealers by the majority of their colleagues in the trade. It is important to note that both of these men are by no means amateurs in the trade and are members of many trade organizations, including the prestigious National Association of Dealers in Ancient, Oriental and Primitive Art (NADAOPA) based in New York and the Antiquities Dealers Association (ADA) based in London. Granted every person has their own faults, and Haber and Veres are probably not perfect angels, but my take on both men was that if they were to be involved in a deal, they would make sure all the letters were crossed and dotted, and that their word could be held with a handshake. Haber, Veres, and Cammarata never gave me the parameters of the deal and I can only speculate as can anyone, as to exactly how the deal was structured between the various parties. It's also noteworthy that Haber, to date, has not offered me any photos or written technical information relative to Steinhardt's vessel, including the weight of the vessel which he could have easily provided, any documents dealing with the authenticity of the vessel, and any other facts concerning the money parameters of the deal. The last point is significant, as this deals with the element of confidentiality between broker and client, and in my opinion, all of this taken together as a whole does lend weight to his credibility as a fair and reputable dealer.

As I began to piece together the mechanics of the deal, I felt certain that Haber was probably unaware, as was Veres, how the piece circulated within Italy and who saw it and when. This was the impression I got from Veres, when I met him in Munich in October of 2002. I also felt certain that the Italian authorities probably assumed that the piece originated within Italian soil, mainly because of Cammarata's relationship with

Manganaro regarding the authenticity of the vessel and the testimony of Vincenzo Pappalardo, a collector living in Catania, who claims he took the piece to Manganaro in 1980 for authentication. If true, then Manganaro did a flip-flop and reversed his opinion about the authenticity of the vessel in 1988.

The Italian authorities, including Aldo de Negri, the assistant magistrate in charge of the case at the Regional Court of Sicily in Termini Imerese, began to complain for the return of the vessel to Italy and shortly thereafter, United States Customs officers closed in on Steinhardt's Fifth Avenue residence in New York and physically entered his home and seized the vessel in November, 1995. Steinhardt had the piece for about four years before it was ripped out of his hands. Once the press and the anti-trade elements learned of the Italian lawsuit to recover the vessel, articles began to appear in the *New York Times, Art & Auction* magazine, and to no one's surprise, *Archaeology* magazine. In short, the obscure Steinhardt was now a household name in the trade and his role as an unknown private collector was now over.

Enraged, and only one week after the gold phiale was seized, Steinhardt hired Frederick R. Schaffer of the firm Schulte Roth & Zabel, who represented him for the return of the vessel from U.S. Customs in U.S. District Court for the Southern District of New York. It wasn't until November of 1997, that U.S. District Judge Barbara S. Jones ruled that the phiale be forfeited and returned to Italy on the grounds that it had been illegally exported from Italy and was unlawfully imported into the United States in 1991. Court documents revealed that the import certificate, otherwise known as the commercial invoice, stated that the country of origin for the vessel was Switzerland and not Italy, and that either Veres and/ or Haber, knowingly or mistakenly, incorrectly filled out the form. Haber later elaborated with me that this technicality was due to the computer software that Haber's custom broker, Jet Air Cargo at JFK International Airport, was using to complete their forms. Haber stated that this software was geared for "modern works of art," and that "the default for the software automatically filled in the blanks," and that "the details for the country of export and the country of origin were not differentiated as they should have been for an object that was an ancient work of art, and the forms were geared for retail products that are of modern manufacture."

Haber further clarified his role with Jet Air Cargo in an article, "The Steinhardt Phiale: a Trading History," which was seen published in *The Art Newspaper* in June 1999. Haber details the following in the article:

"The mistake which has created all the trouble is that the broker stated on the customs entry form, to which he attached the invoice, that the phiale's 'country of origin' was Switzerland. While there is some confusion about precisely what Customs regulations mean by 'country of origin,' I now understand that phrase to refer to the country where the item was manufactured or made. The broker, however, simply stated Switzerland because that was the country from which the phiale was being shipped. The broker later informed me that his computer is programmed so that if the broker forgets to override a default key, the box for country of origin will automatically be filled in with the same information as the country of export, which immediately precedes it on the Customs form. This computer default apparently resulted in the error on the Customs form. In any event, the invoice and other documents show that I certainly did nothing to mislead Customs."

To date, Haber has not taken legal action against Jet Air Cargo, because his legal fees are probably considerable, and this is compounded with the possibility that Jet Air Cargo could have unknowingly made a simple mistake in assuming that their software would place the correct information on the import certificate and that a manual override of the software wasn't necessary to complete the form. Haber later explained to me in October 2001 that, "Had I known about the software, I would have had them fill out the form manually or I would have done it myself."

Court documents also revealed that the value declared for
the vessel on the import certificate was substantially lower than
its true value, but then again in the marketplace in my view, an
object's *current market value* is based on supply and demand,
with a value established and agreed to by both the seller and
the buyer, as it is a collectable. This *current market value* was
not placed on the import certificate, probably because at this
point in time, the vessel had not been tested for authenticity
and its *market value* may have been a combination of its gold
weight value and workmanship value as a modern handicraft
and/or work of art. Therefore, the value of the vessel seen on
the import certificate ($250,000.00) may have, in fact, been a
reflection of the market value of the vessel at the time the import
certificate was drafted, and that not until a sale was
consummated for the vessel could a current market value for
the vessel been established.

Apparently, Judge Jones did not distinguish between these
values, i.e., the *market value* and *current market value*, and
even if she did, she made her ruling primarily based on the
information stated, i.e., the material misstatement on the import
certificate listing Switzerland as the "country of origin" rather
than Italy, and the value declared on the import certificate, and
Haber's invocation of the Fifth Amendment, rather than the
singular issue of Italy considering the phiale as stolen property,
as Italy considers all antiquities to be property of the state and
this would fall under our National Stolen Property Act (NSPA).
Judge Jones's ruling was significant for the antiquities trade,
not because Judge Jones's ruling returned the phiale to Italy,
but rather her ruling avoided the issue of Italy claiming the
phiale as stolen property and this issue has not been fully put
to the test in any United States court.

Shortly after Judge Jones made her ruling, I visited Robert
Haber at his gallery for the first time, as I wanted to view some
pieces that he recently acquired and have a brief discussion
with him about the fate of the vessel. At the time of our meeting,
I had no plans to write this work, but I was interested in

producing a work about the metallurgy of Steinhardt's vessel relative to ancient Greek coinage. I had hoped to gain some technical information regarding the vessel-its weight, size, etc. and fill him in on a theory that I had developed about the vessel. My theory tied in with ancient coinage and could possibly prove that Steinhardt's vessel might have originated outside the modern state of Italy.

Our meeting was cordial, and I expressed an opinion that Italy may not be the vessel's original country of origin and that the testimony garnered by the Italian authorities may have been done so with some pressure involved, and that their witnesses' creditability may not be of the highest regard. I even wrote a letter to Haber to this effect, dated June 7, 1998, and offered the basics of what I knew about the metallurgy of the vessel that I felt was key to the vessel's country of origin. My theory was in the developmental stage and at that time, Haber doubted that it may have been useful to Steinhardt and his attorneys, and in retrospect, I think that he was probably correct in that regard, but it was my hope that this information might be useful to Steinhardt for his appeal. Steinhardt's appeal date was only a few months away and I was sorry that what information I did have at the time would probably not have been of much use to his attorneys.

In November of 1997, Steinhardt's attorneys pursued the argument that Steinhardt was a good faith purchaser and purchased the vessel under Swiss law in Switzerland. Obviously, this argument carried little weight with Judge Jones who ruled against Steinhardt, and this resulted in Steinhardt filing an appeal with the U.S. Court of Appeals for the Second Circuit in Manhattan, which heard arguments from both attorneys on October 14, 1998, and unfortunately for Steinhardt, he subsequently lost his appeal on July 12, 1999.

My argument relative to the metallurgy of the vessel may have made an impact on the case and, as far as I know, it was never considered, probably because my information arrived late on the scene and at the time, my work was in the developmental stage. I was subsequently able to ascertain that the metallurgy was key, in that it would show that the metal that went into the vessel probably did not originate from Sicily, or anywhere else in Italy for that matter. My theory relative to the gold phiale was that in antiquity, at the time the vessel was produced, circa fourth-third century B.C., the most likely and prolific source of precious metal in the ancient Greek world was Mount Pangaeum in northern Greece, near modern-day Kavala. In antiquity during this period, mining activity in Italy and Sicily mainly produced copper, tin, lead, and iron, with some silver and trace amounts of gold. The Etruscans first extensively mined these metals and much later, the Romans further developed and improved upon the mining methods in Italy, but still had to import most, if not all, of their gold for minting coinage in Rome.

Given this fact that the metal that comprises the gold phiale is probably from northern Greece, and coupled with the theory that many artists traveled to work vessels that were votive in nature, point to a strong probability that a foreign artist not native to Magna Graecia (Italy and Sicily) produced the vessel. The Italians were claiming the vessel as cultural patrimony, but my line of thought may have made a claim such as cultural patrimony more difficult, even if the vessel was found in Italy, because in antiquity it was probably produced with metal from northern Greece and likely by an artist foreign to Magna Graecia.

It became apparent to me that the parallels regarding the origins of the phiale mesomphalos and the Decadrachm Hoard are somewhat congruent, and since the Italians were claiming the gold phiale as cultural patrimony, can this loose definition apply to the piece given the facts relative to the metallurgy of the vessel, and the theory that a foreign artist could have produced such a piece, and that the Italians were basing their case on the testimony garnered from individuals that seemed to be under some duress and/or were possibly of questionable repute? In addition, how does the loose definition of cultural patrimony apply to the vessel—does it mean that it is linked to where it was physically found, or where it was originally created in antiquity, or both?

In my initial meeting with Haber, I mentioned this scenario to him and the importance of the metallurgy of the vessel, because it could be scientifically tested and that kind of evidence usually has great weight in a court of law. I explained that the most readily available metal in antiquity was gold coinage, which could be melted down in order to fashion an important votive piece such as a phiale. The use of gold coinage would also give the piece an exact weight range, based on the number of gold coins that went into the vessel, and the fact that ancient gold coinage was minted within a specific weight range, had specific weight standards, and was measured down to few hundredths of a gram. The above facts were only a small part of the mosaic that I was later able to put together relative to my theory about Steinhardt's vessel and I was subsequently able to learn a great deal more about this type of vessel.

I was able to locate another fine example of a gold phiale mesomphalos that is found in the national museum in Sofia, Bulgaria. This vessel has Punic lettering that denotes the value of the piece, based on the *Persic* weight system, and states the number (100) of Persian gold darics/staters that went into the vessel. (See I. Venedikov, *The Panagyurishte Gold Treasure,* Sofia, 1961, p. 22-3.) The weight of this vessel is 845.7 grams, and is an approximate corresponding weight standard of 100 Persian gold darics (the weight norm for a Persian gold daric, circa 450-330 B.C., is 8.35 gm.) and/or 100 gold staters of Lampsakos. (The weight norm for a gold stater of Lampsakos, circa 390-330 B.C., is 8.48 gm.) It is interesting to note that the Punic lettering refers to the Persic weight standard, which was prevalent in the Greek cities of Asia Minor, rather than the *Attic* standard, which was prevalent in the Greek cities of mainland Greece, Italy, and Sicily.

This vessel was also found in a trove of gold vessels in ancient Thrace in Panagyurishte, which is near Sofia in modern

Bulgaria. The location of the find, along with the weight of the vessel corresponding to the inscription seen on the vessel with the known weight standard for the region and period, are both strong indications that a workshop in Thrace could have produced the vessel. Moreover, it is the artistic style of the vessel that is additional evidence that the vessel was produced in ancient Thrace, as the vessel clearly indicates Greek influence and workmanship that is fused with an Oriental form and type. The ancient Greek colony of Lampsakos is a strong possibility for a production site, not only because of the weight standard for the vessel, but more importantly, the geographic location of ancient Lampsakos on the Asiatic side of the Dardanelles, provided the basis for the vessel's artistic style which follows the artistic traditions of both Greece and Asia Minor.

Epigrapher Steven Tracy at Ohio State University examined the Greek lettering seen on Steinhardt's vessel and he concluded that, based on the shape and style of the lettering, the lettering should be dated to circa 300 B.C. If in fact the lettering is authentic, it could be that the lettering was added in antiquity much later than when the vessel was made, which supports my conclusion that the vessel traveled from where it was originally produced, and in addition, the connection to the Greek Attic weight system of the vessel may confirm this. Haber did not reveal the weight of the vessel to me, but if the weight conforms to the Greek Thraco-Macedonian/Attic weight system (the weight norm for an Alexander the Great gold stater that conforms to the Greek Thraco-Macedonian weight standard, circa 330-280 B.C., is 8.6 gm. The extremely rare Greek Attic gold staters, minted circa 300 B.C., also have a weight norm of 8.6 gms.) of 115 gold staters, then the weight of Steinhardt's vessel may be about 989 gms.

It's possible that the weight of the vessel may also confirm the authenticity of the Greek lettering, and if Manganaro made the connection between the type and the descriptive content of the vessel's lettering relative to its weight, this may explain his reversal of opinion regarding the authenticity of the vessel, but this is unlikely, as Andrew Slayman in *Archaeology*, May/June 1998, in "Case of the Golden Phiale," page 38, stated that:

"Sometime after 1983, Manganaro came across a scholarly article about a set of inscribed tablets from the ancient city of Entella, also in Sicily. The tablets contained a pattern of numeration much like that on the phiale, and Manganaro decided that the phiale was authentic."

On the other hand, if the vessel weighs approximately 975 gms or less, then the lettering may refer to the lighter Persic weight standard, and the Attic weight standard referred to in the lettering may not be correct, and consequently, the Greek lettering could be a forgery. If this is the case, could it be that the lettering was recently added so that a reference to the Attic weight system could be seen? However, if the weight of the vessel is approximately 975 gms or less, and the lettering on the vessel is authentic as Steven Tracy maintains, then the lettering probably refers to the lighter Persic weight standard and one could argue this point as further evidence that the vessel was produced in the region where most of these vessels of this type were found, i.e., Bulgaria, Greece, Turkey, and Iran.

A laboratory test (x-ray fluorescence spectrometry) can determine the metal composition of Steinhardt's vessel and may show if any metal originating from the Mount Pangaeum region went into the piece, as certain trace elements in minute quantities have defined percentages, that together, are found in a ratio that is about 98 percent pure gold to about 2 percent of the known combined trace elements. I was able to gather information from several mining companies, relative to the trace metal element combinations and their characteristics, for known mineral deposits and locations in Western Europe. The subsequent gold coinage of Philip II and Alexander the Great may also match the metallurgy of Steinhardt's vessel as noted above, and if so, would be strong evidence to link Steinhardt's vessel as originating in antiquity from a location outside the confines of the modern state of Italy. This scenario is a strong possibility, as the Mount Pangaeum region was rich in mineral resources and was worked by many of the local indigenous natives to the area as early as the sixth century B.C., notably the Bisaltai, the Derrones, and the Orreskioi. These tribes produced a rich coinage that was exported to the Persian Empire, as they produced extremely large denominations such as octadrachms (c. 29.5 gm) and the tremendous dodekadrachm (c. 40.5 gm), with some examples being found as far afield in modern-day Iran, Syria, and Egypt. (See M. Price and N. Waggoner, *Archaic Greek Silver Coinage the Asyut Hoard*, London, 1975.)

It's also probable, because of the rich deposits in the Mount Pangaeum region that the first coin produced on the European mainland came from the area, circa 560-540 B.C. This coin may have been a small silver tribal fraction that depicts a crude crab on the obverse and a rough punch on the reverse. The crab symbol represents a crude and basic Iron Age cycle of life where the local population ate the crabs, and the crabs in turn, ate the excrement of the people. This is a cycle of life that existed in prehistory, perhaps for generations in the Mount Pangaeum region near Lake Bolbe, and was even noted by the Greek historian Herodotus, who is thought to have passed through the region, circa 470-460 B.C.

It's known that Philip II extensively further developed mining of the Mount Pangaeum region and his gold staters (8.6 gms.) were used to expand the Macedonian Empire circa 356-336 B.C. His numerous gold staters, bearing the young bust of Apollo on the obverse and a moving *quadriga* (chariot) on the reverse, transformed a Macedonia, from a loose confederation of independent city states, into a nation that was ready to take on the juggernaut that was the multinational Persian Empire. The heart of his ambition was his coinage, and his principle source of metal was the all-important Mount Pangaeum region. The metal from the region was diffused throughout the ancient Greek world in the form of coinage and, of course, works of art made from precious metal.

When I learned that Steinhardt had lost his appeal, I was certain that if Steinhardt's attorneys had the full and completed corpus of my theory regarding the metallurgy of the vessel in the early stages of their defense, it might have made some impact on the outcome of the trial. The issue of cultural patrimony as to how it would apply to the vessel could have been brought to the forefront relative to the case, along with the authenticity of the vessel itself, and the mechanics of the deal from the Italian side of the fence.

On December 7, 1998, which is a day that will always live with Americans as "a day that will live in infamy," and a little over two years since Judge Jones ruled that the phiale be forfeited back to Italy, the Italian authorities in the Sicilian city of Catania rounded up Manganaro, Cammarata, and a Maurizio Sinistra and extracted testimony from them and even threw Cammarata in jail for fifteen days. (See *Art & Auction*, February 15-28, 1999, page 8, in an article titled, "Antiquities Gang Busted" by Elizabeth Minchilli.) The private collections of Manganaro and Cammarata were seized, although Cammarata was in the process of legally registering his collection according to Italian law. In the heat of the moment, did the Italian authorities consider the possibility that the gold phiale mesomphalos could have been smuggled into Italy from the Balkans, and that the piece may not have been originally found in Italy and/or originally manufactured in Italy? Perhaps more telling is that the Italian authorities needed to shore up the testimony from their witnesses, which they perceived as being needed, in order for them to complete their recovery actions against Steinhardt. At this point in time, the Italian authorities already had Steinhardt's vessel in the hands of United States Customs, but it is also important to note that they now had the private collections of Manganaro and Cammarata in their hands and this was completed prior to the end of Steinhardt's appeal process, which was finalized on July 12, 1999.

The scenario of the vessel coming from the Balkans lends weight to the authenticity of the vessel itself, as virtually most of the known authentic examples of a vessel of this type were found in northern Greece, Bulgaria, and the three principal countries that comprised the former Persian Empire, which is Turkey, Iran, and Iraq. The proximity of these countries to the Mount Pangaeum region and the known export of metal from this region in antiquity, in the form of coinage to these countries is documented. The artistic style of the vessel is also one that is a blend of Greek and Asiatic influence. One could therefore argue, regarding Steinhardt's vessel, that the country of origin in antiquity as being Italy does not lend credibility as to the authenticity of the vessel.

Haber later revealed to me during a second visit to his gallery in October 2001, along with his gallery director, the perceptive Laura Jean Siegel, that Steinhardt's vessel had traces of *microscopic ocean deposits* that were analogous to the deposits seen on the specimen that is seen in the Metropolitan Museum of Art, and if true, would possibly add weight to my theory that Steinhardt's vessel originated in antiquity outside of the modern state of Italy. This would also run counter to the Italian authorities' claim, according to court documents, that Steinhardt's vessel was originally unearthed at a construction site, where a utility company had been digging in Caltavuturo, Sicily, in the 1970s. The ground there is somewhat porous, but I think that if a gold object such as the phiale was buried there for a few thousand years, the patina and the minute mineral deposits working its way into the metal would have been more heavily mineralized, rather than having traces of marine encrustation that has a high degree of salt. In addition, the metal would show signs of *checkering* under high magnification, which is a term used by dealers to describe the molecular breakdown of precious metals that have been subjected to years of burial and mineralization.

Moreover, the gold phiale purchased by the Met in 1962 also had "an encrustation of marine invertebrates on the vessel," and "nothing precise is known of its provenance," as written by Dietrich von Bothmer in the museum's December 1962 issue of the Bulletin; *Bothmer, who in 1962 was the curator of Greek and Roman art. I couldn't help but wonder—could it be that both of these vessels are from the same obscure find, and that Steinhardt's phiale was in an unknown collection, and in an unknown country, or location, for a number of years before it found itself moving up the food chain in Italy?*

Haber further stated that "the Met was satisfied with their tests regarding the authenticity of the vessel," and I understood this to mean that the Met undertook some laboratory tests on the vessel and were satisfied with the results as to its authenticity. I also surmised that Steinhardt probably wouldn't have purchased the vessel unless the Met was first satisfied as to the authenticity of the vessel and this was probably a contingency for the deal between Haber and Steinhardt.

As an added touch, did the Italian authorities consider December 7 as a good day to make their arrests and perhaps send the American collectors, namely Steinhardt, an added message? Did the Italian authorities make their arrests on December 7, 1998, shortly after Steinhardt's attorneys first began their appeal arguments on Oct. 14, 1998, so that they could extract additional testimony from their witnesses that, in their view, could strengthen their case, and were they concerned that their case might be weakened if the "country of origin" issue might materialize, and/or that the vessel or the lettering seen on the vessel might turn out to be a forgery if additional tests were conducted by Steinhardt's attorneys?

The coincidence of the arrest date reminded me of the Hooters restaurant tee shirt that says, *"Delightfully Tacky, Yet Unrefined."*

The "due diligence" that both Haber and Veres had done for the piece is what Steinhardt relied on while he was in the buying mode. Only Haber and Veres knew how reliable the laboratory tests and professional opinions, relative to the authentication of the vessel, actually were, because Haber was the one that probably initiated the vessels first credible laboratory tests, and apparently, nearly everyone involved in this unfortunate affair on the European side of the deal, including the Italian authorities, never extensively addressed the authenticity and vessel's country of origin with a series of legitimate laboratory tests. Due to the fact that there was a considerable amount of money involved in the deal, no one except for Steinhardt, Veres, and especially Haber had a strong interest in the vessel's authenticity, and regarding the "country of origin" issue, court records reveal that Steinhardt's attorneys didn't give the origin of the vessel much consideration, and instead decided to focus on the technicalities of the deal itself. In all fairness to Steinhardt's attorneys, I did not contact Haber until after Judge Jones made her ruling in November of 1997, and at Steinhardt's appeal, I am not aware of Steinhardt's attorneys considering any of the scant information I offered Haber relative to the vessel's country of origin. The scenario of the vessel being produced in antiquity outside of the modern state of Italy may not have been of much use to Steinhardt at the appeal, but at any rate, I thought it was important for all parties involved, in addition to the general public, to have at least been aware of my metallurgical theories regarding the vessel.

The *Steinhardt Affair* sent a chill throughout the trade and put more of an emphasis on "due diligence" that needs to be done prior to a purchase, especially for the more important pieces that are being offered on the market. What should be noted is that Steinhardt's vessel may have been known to some of the Italian authorities in Italy, possibly for a number of years before Veres controlled the piece and as a consequence, more than one dealer in the trade has stated that:

"God only knows who saw it while it was there, and collectors should take care with pieces that are offered that have been *through the mill.*"

This is a term that many dealers refer to when a piece has been seen by a number of people in the market and unfortunately for Haber, this is the position taken by many dealers in the trade as to how he handled the deal with Steinhardt. In reality, I think Haber, and to some degree Veres, have taken some unfair criticism from many of their colleagues in the trade, and to their credit and not fully realized by many of their colleagues is that Haber and Veres were probably not aware of the vessel being in Italy for a number of years, if in fact it was in Italy for a number of years, the vessel's complete chain of ownership in Italy, who saw the vessel while it was in Italy, and exactly what the Italian authorities knew about the vessel relative to the authenticity and the vessel's country of origin. One can take this a step further, because after the deal was consummated for the vessel and the money flowed to the Italian side of the deal, at this point it became uncertain to know exactly how the money was divided and who got what. Did they squabble over the money and decide to turn on one another and bring the Italian authorities into the picture at this point?

One fact that either Haber and/or Veres may or may not have been aware of was the scenario that the Italian authorities may have considered the vessel to be a fake while it was in Italy, if in fact the vessel was in Italy for a considerable amount of time, and if this was the case, then the Italian authorities never considered it to be authentic until it left Italy and a deal for the vessel was consummated. In this scenario, the Italian authorities did a 180 in their thinking. This may also explain why the Italian authorities didn't act sooner to recover the vessel while it supposedly was in Italy for a considerable amount of time, unless of course, some individuals who saw the vessel prior to it leaving Italy never got paid, in one way or another, and decided to cooperate with the Italian authorities who then became fully aware of the vessel, or it may be, as one New York dealer adeptly speculated, that it was a chance for the Italian authorities to strike at the heart of the American collecting market with much fanfare and a much publicized seizure, and it was not in the Italian authorities' best interests whether the vessel was authentic or a forgery, but rather that the vessel *left* the country and *entered* the market. It would be interesting to know if the Italian authorities would allow additional independent laboratory tests, not only to determine its authenticity, but also the metallurgy of the vessel so that it could be compared to other extant specimens and the data that I have compiled relative to the metallurgy of ancient Greek coinage.

Whatever the case, Steinhardt ended up losing his *Maltese Falcon* which was a complete surprise to him, and in the end, Steinhardt did us all a favor, because dealers are now being more careful as to who they are buying from and collectors are now considering more "due diligence" before they buy. This is a good thing, because another *Steinhardt Affair* might be avoided.

And what of the collectors that are considering registering their collections in Italy? In all probability, they have moved their collections underground and/or out of the country, because who can blame them? For leaving their collections in Italy opens up the possibility that they will be seized and with them locked in Italy, their collections are virtually worthless on the international market. Many of these Italian collectors who have, in many cases, owned their collections for more than one generation may not have documents that prove that they have owned their collections before 1902, and without the proper documentation, their collections are subject to seizure by the Italian authorities. The much-publicized *Steinhardt Affair* has insured that the majority of Italian collectors are now aware of the Italian law and the seizure of the Italian collections within Italy, and now, the Italian authorities will have to contend with this more than ever, so in the end, did they come out on top even if they gained the golden phiale mesomphalos? Considering the fact that the Italian collectors are now quietly moving hundreds of their objects out of the country, only history can be the judge, and unfortunately for Italy as a whole, the Italian authorities that are seizing these old collections that have no documentation may also have lost sight of the true meaning of *Senatus Populusque Romanus* (S.P.Q.R.).

Author's note: In June 2002, I was finally able to learn the technical information relative to Steinhardt's vessel, otherwise now known as the *Phiale of Achyris*. I found that the vessel has a height of 4 cm, a diameter of 23 cm, and a weight of approximately 982 grams. In contrast, the phiale at the Met has a height of 3.6 cm, a diameter of 23.5 cm, and a weight of approximately 748 grams.

The *Phiale of Achyris* probably conforms to the Greek Thraco-Macedonian/Attic weight system, with a weight norm of 8.6 grams for a gold stater. It should be noted that this weight standard became "degraded" or lighter regarding the vast *posthumous* gold coinage of Alexander the Great, circa 323-280 b.c., with the majority of gold staters having a weight range of approximately 8.5-8.6 grams. If the Greek lettering on the vessel is authentic as Stephen Tracy maintains, with a dating to circa 300 b.c., then the average weight per gold stater that is referred to in the lettering is approximately 8.54 grams. It should also be noted that the *posthumous* coinage of Alexander the Great was mostly mass produced regal issues that largely replaced autonomous coins of individual Greek cities throughout Asia Minor, and the metallurgy from these issues may match the metallurgy of the *Phiale of Achyris*, so the question remains—*whose cultural patrimony is being stolen in the first place and how legitimate is the Italian claim for the Phiale of Achyris in the name of cultural patrimony, but more importantly, how does the loose definition of cultural patrimony apply to the vessel—does it mean that it is linked to where it is physically found, or where it was originally created in antiquity, or both?*

CHAPTER FOURTEEN

The Schultz Case

History is now propelling the antiquities trade into new territory. Like the episodes noted in this work, perhaps the most important episode that will determine the future of the trade is now developing, and its outcome will forever shape the future for all parties involved. According to William G. Pearlstein, a New York attorney who represents the National Association of Dealers in Ancient, Oriental and Primitive Art (NADAOP), has stated the following:

"This could be the big one. If the government wins this case, then every dealer, collector, and museum that owns an object without proper export documents is risking that the government may consider that object as stolen property."

The case centers around New York gallery owner Frederick Schultz, who went on record regarding the provenance of the pieces that were seized from Giacomo Medici in Geneva. He was charged by Mary Jo White, the U.S. Attorney for the Southern District of New York, on July 16, 2001, on one count of conspiring with an unnamed confederate to "possess, conceal, store, barter, sell and dispose of" Egyptian artifacts that the government claims were stolen from Egypt.

The circumstances of the case evolve around a "Co-conspirator 1," this according to the indictment against Schultz, who traveled throughout Egypt acquiring antiquities from the locals and then sold or consigned objects to Schultz, who allegedly knew the activities of "Co-conspirator 1" and was fully aware of their origin and created false provenance for the pieces in question from 1991 to 1995. This was in violation of Egypt's law 117, which mandates that all antiquities found after 1983 within the country are state-owned and cannot be traded, transferred, or privately owned. In addition, all antiquities privately owned prior to 1983 are to be registered and recorded, and antiquities without proper documentation are subject to seizure.

The government is basing its case on the testimony of this "Co-conspirator 1," who is thought to be Jonathon Tokeley-Parry, an antiquities dealer from Idesleigh, United Kingdom. The government's use of a material witness is parallel to the witnesses utilized by the Italian government in the Steinhardt case, and the lead attorney for Schultz, Linda Imes, of the New York firm Richards, Spears, Kibbe & Orbe, has gone on record in the *New York Times* on July 17, 2001, in an article titled "Indictment Alleges Dealer Held Ancient Art Illegally": "We strongly deny the charges in the indictment. We strongly deny that Mr. Schultz ever knew that any antiquity he received, purchased, or sold to any person was stolen from the nation of Egypt or anyone else."

The Schultz case may test the court ruling, *United States v. McClain*, which upheld the conviction in 1977 of an appraiser, Patty McClain, who was prosecuted for "conspiring to transport" pre-Columbian objects from Mexico into Texas. The court ruling relied on Mexican law that defined what constituted stolen property, and arguably, circumvented and superseded current U.S. law at the time. Imes further has gone on the record in the *New York Times* in the article noted above that the U.S. government is "pursuing Mr. Schultz on an arcane legal theory on which the government's charges are based is without merit."

Several lawyers close to the case are concerned that the U.S. government is opening up a dangerous precedent of legal law that, in effect, stipulates that a crime against Egypt is a crime against America and that an American court of law should fully uphold and enforce an Egyptian law. The Steinhardt case avoided this scenario, with Judge Jones ruling that the import certificate was improperly filed out and was grounds for the U.S. Customs and the Italian authorities to seize the vessel. The idea of a foreign government, such as Egypt, with its laws applying to U.S. citizens here at home does not sit well with most people that are familiar with the case, and it would be interesting to see if any of the anti-trade individuals, that are U.S. citizens, come forward and condemn this line of reasoning of the U.S. Attorney's office. There is some speculation that the U.S. Attorney's office may avoid this as well, and would instead concentrate on the objects themselves and their witnesses that are involved in the case, since the United States and New York have recently been attacked by foreign terrorists on September 11, 2001 and most Americans are not currently sympathetic to foreign laws that may apply to U.S. citizens here at home.

There is additional speculation that the pro-trade individuals are hoping that the U.S. Attorney's office *does* take this course of action, because in the current political environment with the United States in a state of war against terrorism, a New York jury would not look favorable on this scenario of a foreign law applying to U.S. citizens and would probably overwhelmingly rule in favor of Schultz, which would kill off any future court action that would involve *United States v. McClain.*

The outcome of this case is critical to the future of the antiquities trade. If the court rules against Schultz, the *Schultz case* could open up a floodgate of legal action against museums, dealers, and collectors, or if *United States v. McClain* is not utilized by the U.S. Attorney's office and a ruling goes against Schultz, then some middle ground might be achieved regarding the trade, but the specter of *United States v. McClain* would remain in place.

There is also additional speculation, from those close to the *Schultz Case*, that this case is a test case on behalf of the

Egyptian government to gain the return of the Rosetta Stone from the British Museum, discovered in 1799 and in the British Museum since 1802. The Egyptian Minister of Culture, Farouk Hosni, stated in late 1995 that Egypt might route an appeal for the return of the Rosetta Stone through the United Nations Educational, Scientific and Cultural Organization (UNESCO).

Dr. Zahi Hawass, Director of the Pyramids, Giza, and Director of Egypt's Supreme Council of Antiquities has also stated that:

"The return of the Rosetta Stone is considered a fair request, and UNESCO agreements give us this right."

Dr. Hawass has also gone on record to take on cultural institutions worldwide, in order to return fragments of the Temple of Seti, and declared in *Newsweek*, September 2, 2002, in an article titled "Tomb Raiders, Beware!" by Gretel Kovach:

"When they know that I am serious, that I plan to rebuild the temples *in situ,* how could they refuse? What about the institutions that won't cooperate? I'll post their names on the Internet! I'll take them to court! No scientific cooperation!"

In response to the *Schultz Case,* Dr. Hawass has also permanently barred one British and one American archaeologist from working in Egypt for defending Schultz. (See *Newsweek,* ibid above, page 40.) One could possibly say that the issue of cultural patrimony has finally gone the full circle, and has finally come to impact not only those involved in the antiquities trade from a marketing standpoint, but also those from a scientific standpoint, including the archaeologists.

The Egyptian quest to recover the Rosetta Stone also opens up the possibility of other foreign governments that may follow suit, including Greece's request for the Elgin Marbles from the British Museum and the Venus de Milo from the Louvre. The implications of the Schultz Case could be such that many foreign governments could exercise their political nationalism and go on a rampage, demanding the return of objects from the individual collector, to the most prestigious cultural institutions in our country, such as the Metropolitan Museum in New York. This will drive the trade underground, and very few people will see collections that are held privately, and the public institutions in our country will suffer greatly, because no one will donate their collections for fear that they may be seized.

When I met with Frederick Schultz in October 2001, he seemed optimistic that he would win his case and that all of the government's charges against him were unfounded. *I also brought up the scenario that since he went on record in defining the provenance of many of the pieces that were seized in the Geneva Seizure, did the U.S. government have an agenda to go after him in one way or another?*

His answer to this was calm, rational, and quickly thought out, "No, I don't think this is the case, and it's hard to say what the U.S. Attorney's office is thinking."

Looking back at my brief moments with Schultz I couldn't help but think that perhaps there is more to this than meets the eye, because in addition to his public comments regarding the pieces seized from Giacomo Medici in the Geneva Freeport, three years earlier on October 9, 1998, in the *New York Times* in an article titled "Ancient Art Stirs Landmark Court Battle," Schultz went on public record by commenting on the Steinhardt case as the current president of the National Association of Dealers in Ancient, Oriental and Primitive Art (NADAOPA). He stated the following: "Customs over the past few years has exceeded their mandate very seriously, and the Steinhardt case is one example. They're shooting from the hip, and these people have a lot of power."

With these public comments regarding U.S. Customs and the Internet site (http://www.archaeology.org/online/features/geneva/index.html) that explained his viewpoint relative to the provenance of the pieces seized in the Geneva Seizure, I couldn't help but think that Schultz had become a political target of sorts, and are his current legal problems somehow tied in with his outspoken opinions?

In a recent development in November 2001, the Archaeological Institute of America (AIA) has petitioned the judge that is hearing the *Schultz case* in order to file an amicus brief. In support of the AIA is the Society for American Archaeology, the Society for Historical Archaeology, the American Anthropological Association, and the U.S. National Committee of the International Council on Monuments and Sites. It's interesting to note that all of these organizations are allied against Schultz concerning his case, and seem to be in favor of the US recognizing Egyptian laws applying to U.S. citizens like Schultz. One attorney familiar and close to the case commented:

"It's scary that what we have here is all of these prestigious U.S. cultural organizations, with all of their power, money, and influence all allied against Schultz, and are all apparently in support of *foreign* laws that would apply to U.S. citizens here at home. These *foreign* laws could impact and impinge on several civil liberties that all Americans now have a right to enjoy, such as collecting art, and all this is an effort to protect archaeological sites worldwide from looters. If this is the tradeoff, I think I would rather want my civil liberties protected, and this is really what is important to me as an American citizen. What do you think?"

William Pearlstein, a lawyer for the National Association of Dealers in Ancient, Oriental and Primitive Art (NADAOPA) perhaps summed up the pro-trade position concerning the Schultz Case in the *New York Times* on January 30, 2002, in an article "Illicit Antiquities and a Case Fit for Solomon" by Celestine Bohlen:

"What the United States is doing is quite radical and quite to the contrary of the interest of museums, the public, the dealers, and the auction houses. I think the government is out to squelch the antiquities trade, and no one is taking into account the interest of the public it serves."

Through all of this, I have not lost sight at what is still important to me and I am sure that there are other collectors that feel the same way, and that is the simple enjoyment of the pieces themselves. Art can be a great way for people to draw closer together and in my mind, this is far more important than seeing, who-gets-what, and who-wins-what, and this is perhaps what the anti-trade elements have missed in their zeal to claim, who-gets-what, and who-wins-what. In these times when terror has touched all of us in the USA, the enjoyment of the art is a nice diversion and should continue on both a private and public basis, regardless whether Schultz is found guilty or not and what the outcome of the trial may be.

Author's note: On January 3, 2002, Judge Jed Rakoff denied Linda Imes's petition to dismiss the case, and in February convicted Schultz on a single count of *conspiring* to sell Egyptian antiquities in violation of the U.S. National Stolen Property Act (NSPA), rather than the *actual theft* of Egyptian antiquities. The government was able to convince a jury that the Egyptian pieces in question, notably a stone bust of Amenhotep III from the fourteenth century B.C., were recently stolen from Egypt, and that Schultz agreed to help Tokeley-Parry sell one of the sixteen "stolen" pieces for a conspiracy to exist. The government's star witness, Tokeley-Parry, was a convicted smuggler who was charged in 1997 by Scotland Yard and sentenced to six years in a U.K. prison.

Schultz appealed the ruling and subsequently lost his appeal on June 25, 2003. It remains to be seen how the *Schultz Case* may impact the worldwide antiquities trade, but one thing is certain, the private owners of antiquities in the "art-rich" countries will probably move their collections even further from view, and not allow any academics to view, photo, and document their collections, as this may expose their collections for possible seizure. The same scenario will probably apply here at home, as more and more *private* collections become more *private.*

I also think there is now a new movement among collectors, in that they now regard the issue of "provenance" as being moot, because they now have a sense that they are being driven underground due to the current political climate in the market and the constant mantra from the archaeological community calling for the return of objects back to the "art-rich" countries. A great many collectors are now simply buying what they like and in the process, their collections are even more *private* than they were before. This is unfortunate, because the real losers are the American people and our cultural institutions, as collectors will donate less and less and a broader range of people will not be able to view pieces that could have been seen in a different political environment. Ultimately, it may be up to the US Congress to step in and reform the current laws that are now on the books in order to protect the *private* collector and *private* property here in the US, and hopefully, any new legislation would balance out against those foreign laws that are protectionist in nature.

CHAPTER FIFTEEN

Finding the Middle Ground

Our nation is now at a crossroads in history and the state of the nation and the resolve of our people is what will make all the difference regarding the future of the antiquities trade and more importantly, the survival of our republic. Let us not forget the lessons learned from ancient history, and the determination and the fortitude of ancient Athens comes to mind in the following passage from Herodotus—Book VI, 115:

"The Persians, seeing the attack developing at the double, prepared to meet it, thinking it suicidal madness for the Athenians to risk an assault with so small a force—rushing in with no support from either cavalry or archers. Well, that was what they imagined: nevertheless, the Athenians came on, closed with the enemy all along the line, and fought in a way not to be forgotten. They were the first Greeks, so far as I know, to charge at a run, and the first who dared to look without flinching at Persian dress and the men who wore it; for until that day came, no Greek could hear even the word Persian without terror."

This passage describing the Athenian victory over the Persians at Marathon was perhaps the greatest military victory in the face of overwhelming adversity. The Battle of Marathon was won through courage, skill of arms, and the use of heavy body armor. The light dress of the Persians was no match for the heavily armed Greek *hoplites* (citizen soldiers) that struck a lightning attack, and unexpectedly ran in an elongated line headfirst into the camp of the Persians during the early morning hours. Some military experts have speculated that the Athenians were outnumbered by five-to-one. The Athenian general, Miltiades, undoubtedly realizing that the hoplite heavy body armor was a major factor in the stunning Athenian victory, is said after the battle to have dedicated his helmet to Zeus at Olympia. A Corinthian type helmet found during excavations at Olympia bears the inscription on the left cheek-piece, "Miltiades presented this to Zeus."

The helmet is an antiquity that tells a story, and in this case, the story was one that shaped the future of our western democratic society. The future of the antiquities trade was, and is, greatly influenced by some of the events noted in this work, but the trade is one that evolves, and is one that is meeting some of the expectations of both ends of the spectrum, from the dealers and collectors, who tend to support an open and free market that follows the concept of English common property law, to the archeologists and politicians, who tend to support a complete ban on the trade and follow the concept of state ownership of property. To expect a complete ban on the trade is unrealistic and pure fantasy, as there are hundreds of documented pieces with clear provenance that are currently being bought and sold on the international market every day, in addition to the pieces that are not documented and have been in private collections, and in many cases, for several generations. There are obviously an unknown number of pieces offered in the marketplace that are fresh out of the dirt, but to label all antiquities offered in the marketplace as such is not only due to a lack of knowledge about the trade, but more likely, these statements encompass a political agenda that is behind this sort of speculation.

This work has focused on the trade from the dealers and collectors' point of view, and admittedly, that is the prevailing position taken, but in retrospect, this work has also brought to light some of the concerns of those that want the trade curtailed and banned, and their positions in many cases are not without merit. There is no question that there are many archaeological sites worldwide that are suffering damage through tourism and looting, but to tie this exclusively to the trade is not only unfounded, but more often than not, it is again a political and/ or economic agenda that is the face behind the mask. The trade has without question imbued objects with value, and as such, has contributed to their survival and their continued preservation, and the preservation of objects is the main concern of the private collector.

Perhaps an even greater threat to the preservation of antiquities is tied to the many governments themselves that are losing their ability to care for their myriad of objects in their cultural institutions, because it takes millions of dollars each year to staff and pay salaries, lighting, heating, cleaning, etc. Giuliano Urbani, Italy's minister of culture, has recently stated in the *New York Times* on December 3, 2001 that:

"Right now thirty percent of our artistic heritage is in storage-and slightly dubious storage, because we have so much of it, we can't afford to get it out of the basement."

Italy is now forming legislation to privatize many of its museums in order to get the cost of managing these institutions off the books of the country's national budget. Private management is the primary attribute of the private collector, who finds it essential to preserve his or her collection by taking the time, money, and effort to do so. It's interesting to note that Italy is now pursuing this course of action, but what form will this process take, and in the end, down what road will this lead? In the not-too-distant future, will we be seeing huge lighted billboards displaying soft drink advertisements, unrestricted gate admission, and increased pollution at pristine archaeological sites such as Pompeii?

The unchecked governmental commercialization of archaeological sites is perhaps an issue that both the "pro" and "anti" antiquities trade groups should be focusing on, rather than the recently contested who-gets-what issue. The pristine eighth century Buddhist monument Borobudur in central Java is now in the minds of many Indonesian government officials as a way for them to create fast cash through commercial development. Governor Mardiyanto of central Java wants to build a shopping mall titled *Java World*, and plans for this project reveal its location at the gateway to the monument, along with a tramway that can take tourists from the mall to the base of the monument itself. Unfortunately, the foundations of this grand multi-terraced monument, with its hundreds of seated Buddha statues, are sinking year by year and development of this sort could possibly endanger the monument even more. (See *New York Times*, February 27, 2003, p. A4 "Buddhist Monument and Mall: Will Twain Meet?)

The Borobudur site in 1991 was designated by UNESCO as a "World Heritage Site," a designation that is supposed to protect it from commercial intrusions and development. This is important because no one really knows why the monument was built where it is today and what purpose it could have served, as there are no rooms that provided sanctuary for worship and/or ceremony. I think that the monument, as well as the surrounding countryside, was in itself a temple for the many Buddhist pilgrims that visited the site, and it was this serene splendor that perhaps was the impetus for its creation. It's sad that in the case of Borobudur, the government of Indonesia may have lost sight of this Buddhist thought of perception and is exploring the idea of extensive commercial development of the site. The global governmental commercialization of ancient archaeological sites over the next century could be the most dangerous threat relative to the survival of ancient art, and the development plans for Borobudur may only be the beginning.

In the end, we all have to find a common ground in order to preserve what art and archaeological sites there is now, as well as what may be found in the future, and the sensationalist articles such as those seen in *Connoisseur, Art & Auction,* and *Archaeology Magazine* is not the answer, and if anything, they have inflamed the political scene and have damaged the few opportunities that could have contributed in advancing some common ground between both ends of the spectrum. For all of us that are involved in the trade, in one way or another, we all must continue to work together so that some common ground in the marketplace can be achieved, and as such, many more objects may be preserved for future generations. Finding the middle ground is the nexus of the democratic traditions of our great country, and like Miltiades, we must find the courage to do so and move forward.

Author's note: On April 11 and 12, 2003, hundreds of looters sacked the Iraqi National Museum in Baghdad and made off with thousands of objects that date from the dawn of civilization. After the looters pillaged government buildings and businesses after the collapse of Saddam Hussein's regime, they targeted the museum, leaving broken objects and picking most of the display cases clean of any objects. What remains unclear at the time of the looting is whether any of the museum's employees were under the pay of the regime that may have helped this event move forward, how many objects were in fact in the hands of members of Saddam's inner circle and/or on display outside of the museum, if any duplicate fakes were at the museum in place of their originals, and if there were any professionals involved shortly before and during the mass looting that took place. Shortly after the looting took place, Dr. Jerry Eisenberg, a founding member of the International Association of Dealers in Ancient Art, stated in *USA Today* on April 15, 2003, that "the antiquities dealers association is urging its 200 members worldwide to avoid buying anything Iraqi that is not provenanced, meaning any object that does not have a clear record of its origin and ownership over time."

It's this author's hope that many of these objects will be recovered, and that both ends of the spectrum, i.e., those that are both positive and negative regarding the trade may finally work together in saving those objects that define the early condition of man and civilization as we know it.

APPENDIX

Selected Documents

The *Geneva Seizure* Internet site (http://www.archaeology.org/online/features/geneva/index.html) is maintained by *Archaeology* magazine and was written by Andrew Slayman, associate Editor of *Archaeology*.

The *Geneva Seizure* Internet site has commentary regarding a partial list of photos that were taken by Swiss and Italian authorities during the seizure.

A response to this commentary is in the form of a letter that was addressed to *Archaeology* magazine and Andrew Slayman by Frederick Schultz, who was at the time his letter was drafted, the acting president of the National Association of Dealers in Ancient, Oriental and Primitive Art (NADAOPA).

An additional response to the commentary, seen on the *Geneva Seizure* Internet site, and the events concerning the *Geneva Seizure* is from Giacomo Medici.

It should be noted that the 68 photos seen in the *Geneva Seizure* Internet site is only a fraction of the myriad of photos that were taken during the seizure, but they still reveal a great many of the pieces seized at the Geneva Freeport. Perhaps more revealing, the photos define the various cultures that produced the pieces and often show various auction identification tags that are seen attached to many of the pieces.

It remains questionable as to how long the *Geneva Seizure* Internet site will be on the Internet. The following letters are the responses to the *Geneva Seizure* Internet site by Frederick Schultz and Giacomo Medici:

National Association of Dealers in Ancient,
Oriental & Primitive Art

June 16, 1998

To: Archaeology Magazine
From: Frederick Schultz, President

After reading Peter Watson's *Sotheby's: The Inside Story* and myriad subsequent magazine articles about the renowned antiquities kingpin, Giacomo Medici, I was thrilled to be able to see the images posted on your website "Geneva Seizure," which purports to display "10,000 artifacts, most of them probably smuggled from Italy."

Instead of proving that Mr. Medici is the secret smuggling connection from Italy, however, your website proved exactly the opposite, and proved it beyond a shadow of a doubt. With the exception of the Ostia column capitals, every object of possible Italian provenience comes from a bona fide old collection. My comments refer to the photos as numbered on the website:

3. Griffin protome—Thetis collection, Sotheby's London, 8 July 1991, #267.
7. Two gold plaques with auction tags visible— Sotheby's London.

10. Boetian terra-cotta—Erlenmeyer collection, Sotheby's London, 9 July 1990, #50.

26. Attic black-figure cup—auction at Summa Gallery, Beverly Hills, 1981; Hunt collection, Sotheby's New York, 19 June 1990, #3.

32. Relief of marching warriors (fake)—the relief is a genuine East Greek object, also from auction, and the other relief fragments in the image are Egyptian, Sotheby's London, 8 July 1991, #162 and #165.

42. Flask and zoomorphic vase—the vase is Mycenean, not Italian.

43. Etruscan bronze candelabrum—Thetis collection, #270. The bronze column in the image is an auction object, too. Note the auction tag.

44. Cypriot pottery—the pair of vases are not at all Cypriot. They are Urartu (Near Eastern), exSotheby's, 1993 (?).

49. Opus sectile (fake)—This is not an imitation of an ancient object, but a perfectly normal contemporary table top.

50. Minoan jar—Erlenmeyer collection, Sotheby's London, 9 July 1990, #154.

51. Grave relief and Herakles statue—the relief is Greek, ex-Sotheby's London. The "Herakles" is a fragment from an Egyptian limestone figure of a priest wearing the leopard skin, and also comes from auction.

55. Rhodian pottery—never found in Italy.

59-60. Romano-British objects—all bearing Sotheby's tags; never found in Italy.

63. Attic red-figure cup—Hunt collection, # 11.

64. Attic red-figure hydria—Hunt collection, # 13.

66. Roman wall painting—from a private Swiss collection.
67. Greek Geometric and Mycenaen objects—all bearing Sotheby's tags; never found in Italy.

The other photos represent objects of no discernible art-historical importance, aesthetic appeal, or commercial value. I do not doubt that many once came from tombs. However, it is highly unlikely that an American museum would accept them even as donations. What is especially ironic is that many of the "stolen" objects came from two notable Swiss collections, Thetis and Erlenmeyer, sold at public auction.

The ignorance and misinformation of your website is plainly embarrassing for a magazine that claims to defend science and truth. Although I have never met Mr. Medici and cannot vouch for him, I note that his arrest in Italy was not followed by any prosecution, and that he won his case outright in Swiss Federal Court. Afterwards, the Italians then mounted a diplomatic campaign against him, prevailing upon the Swiss authorities to extend the seizure. Having failed in a court of law, the Italians then apparently leaked their photos to you, ARCHAEOLOGY, who are conducting a kangaroo court of your own.

—

ARCHEOLOGY

For the attention of Mr. Andrew SLAYMAN

Dear Sir,

Some of my friends told me about an article which appeared in the journal Archeology. This article has appeared in full on Internet.

Thank you very much. This article makes it possible, for the first time in 3 years to defend myself against accusations completely without foundation.

None of those accusing me gave me any possibility to defend myself. On 13 September 1995, I was subjected to a search at the Geneva free port. I cannot deny that it was violent and rough!

I have the right to claim that the norms guaranteeing a standard search procedure were not observed at that stage. Indeed, operations took place without a representative of the company being present, or even myself. No INVENTORY either of objects or of documents showing the lawful source of the objects was made.

These documents not having been "FOUND", the objects were nonetheless photographed. This photo "ALBUM" was to "REPLACE" the inventory. But the photographs do not represent "IN FULL" the objects which were inside the premises! What does this fact mean? Why were some objects not photographed? Do I have the right, at present, to know if these objects were inside the premises? When I say that I was not given any possibility to defend myself, I want to point out that my presence or that of a lawyer representing the company would have avoided stating that during the search no document dealing with the lawful origin of the objects was found! These documents were there and I cannot be accused, at present, of any manipulation if the police did not see them and did not find them.

It is not necessary, at this point, to go any further. The documents in my possession which should have demonstrated the lawful origin of all the objects were not found: therefore, the whole procedural argument has been completely distorted.

I do not wish to accuse anyone; it is not up to me to make sure that all the rights of a citizen "under investigation" have been respected; I only with to bring to public opinion the knowledge that the facts brought out at the Geneva free port were not those reported in the newspapers and on television throughout the world.

The "monster" who should have exported 10,000 items illegally does not exist; "Ali Baba's cave" does not exist; it is not true what Peter Watson states that Sotheby's of London accepted in fill knowledge and for sale illicit objects coming from Italy.

The contrary is true! Sotheby's knew, because they had viewed them before, that all the objects came lawfully from old Swiss and European collections.

Presently, after nearly 3 years, 68 photographs taken inside the premises of the free port which reproduce the sequestered objects appear on Internet. How can such an action be justified?

We are still in the INVESTIGATIVE phase. Why can reserved documents, covered by secret of investigation be shown on Internet? Is all this normal?

From an examination of the photographs, it can easily be deducted [sic] that many of the objects are not of Italic origin; it can be scientifically demonstrated that most of these objects could not have been found in Italian archeological sites! Why then does one continue to claim and repeat that these are of Italian origin? Many objects still carry labels attesting to their origin, why don't the archeologists point out this very important fact?

I bought the objects from the same sources where the most important museums in the world and private collectors buy. The objects which are still sequestered in the Geneva free port come from LAWFUL sources, from important collections and were bought for an equitable price. None were received. Many persons can testify that they saw me in the world's main auction houses, while I bought at competitive prices the objects now sequestered in the Geneva free port.

The idea is to impress public opinion by announcing that the seizure was of 10,000 items. This is not true! How could this number be reached if no inventory were made? The declared value is 35 million dollars; who would buy these objects even at half of that price?

Besides the number of perhaps 200/300 items, no one in America among museums and private collectors would be willing to buy most of the sequestered items at the Geneva free port, in particular at present when this defamatory campaign has been carried out against me. To then say nothing about my health. [sic]

I hope, one day, not too far away, that everything will be cleared up and that all the items presently taken away from me will be recognised and returned to me.

Please, in case my present letter is accepted, publish it IN FULL.

I am completely at your disposal to explain any point that you have not yet understood.

Being sure that an event similar to mine would have never happened in America, I reserve my rights to take action for damages against any author of violations of the law, no one excluded; please accept my most grateful thanks.

Kind regards,